I love Bruce!

CONTENTIOUS COUNSEL:

How the world's most reviled industry turned obstacles into opportunity and what your business can learn about navigating a combative, litigious, and regulated world.

By Max A Krangle, BSc, LLB

Former General Counsel
R. J. Reynolds Global Products

Former Assistant General Counsel
Japan Tobacco International

CounselStrategy.com

©2023 by Max Krangle

WARNING: ALWAYS BE OPEN TO THE POSSIBILITY THAT YOU MIGHT BE WRONG.

ISBN: 9798391906247

DEDICATION

To my incredible wife, Melany. You selflessly allowed your career to give way to mine, followed me around the world, gave birth to our two amazing daughters, and always believed in me. I couldn't have done any of this without you.

ACKNOWLEDGEMENTS

To my parents, Bill and Eva, who gave me the gift of becoming a lawyer.

To Tom Rivers at ABC News, an exceptional journalist, mentor and radio pirate.

To Jens Hills, an extraordinary lawyer who gave me my first chance and schooled me in legal practice.

To Suzanne Wise, for teaching me much of what I know about corporate culture.

To Yann Tardif & Cesar Prieto, two marketing OGs that took the time to teach me.

To the late Guy Blynn, my mentor and friend. Gone too soon, but never forgotten.

To Josh Knelman, for bringing my tobacco journey to life.

Photo Credit: Giovanni Capriotti

TABLE OF CONTENTS

Preface 1
Introduction: Smoking Kills 7
Chapter 1: You've Come a Long Way Baby 17
Chapter 2: Stealing the Playbook 45
Chapter 3: Fewer Customers, More Profits 53
Chapter 4: What They Don't Teach You In Business School 69
Chapter 5: Tax Me More, Please 83
Chapter 6: Don't Fear Regulation 99
Chapter 7: Engaging in Candid Dialogue 109
Chapter 8: Governance Starts From Within 129
Chapter 9: Your Most Important Asset: Your Employees 141
Chapter 10: Always Manage Your Risk, Always 165
Chapter 11: Coping with Stress 187
Conclusions:
Accept What is Thrown at You 205
About the Author 219
Legal Notice 227

PREFACE

Here's the news: I am going to sue the Brown & Williamson Tobacco Company, manufacturers of Pall Mall cigarettes, for a billion bucks. Starting when I was only twelve years old, I have never chain-smoked anything but unfiltered Pall Malls. And for many years now, right on the package, Brown & Williamson have promised to kill me. But I am eighty-two. Thanks a lot, you dirty rats. The last thing I ever wanted was to be alive when the three most powerful people on the whole planet would be named Bush, Dick and Colon.
- Kurt Vonnegut

Here's the thing. There is a huge difference between "could," "could very well," "likely will," "probably will," "may," and just simply "will." No one has ever guaranteed anyone that they would die from smoking. It may be a contributing factor to their death, but it may not be *the* factor. Mr. Vonnegut, a chain-smoker, made it to his eighty-fifth year. It was reported at the time that he died "as a result of brain injuries incurred several weeks prior, from a fall at his brownstone home." As you will learn, tobacco can result in some 250 plus illnesses and diseases. Falling in one's home is not one of them.

Many people have no doubt said, one way or another, "If I had only known I would have lived this long I would have taken better care of myself," and so they should have. Smoking is rude. Smoking is disgusting. Smoking kills. You should not smoke. But that does not mean you cannot learn from the industry, which, after all, is one hundred percent legal. And, as long as your business is as well, I am here to teach you some things you probably have never heard before. This book truly does come under the heading "things they don't teach in business school."

I would like to think of this book as a bridge between impression and reality. A lot of what you believe about the tobacco industry is wrong; a lot is correct. But this is a business book. While you will learn about tobacco, you did not buy this book, and you are not reading it, to become an expert on an ancient cash crop. You want to learn the lessons of the tobacco industry and how you can apply them to have a successful company.

There are many things you are about to learn. Some of you probably already know, but it is nevertheless important to be reminded of them. Many business owners want to be "unicorns" or industrial "black swans." That's all fine and good, but what you don't want to be is an "ostrich," bearing your head in the sand hoping that your problems will disappear. Problems rarely disappear; they usually get worse.

CONTENTIOUS COUNSEL

Perhaps the most important business lesson you were ever taught came from your mother (or father): Don't lie. Telling the truth is the simplest response to critics. As soon as you agree with someone, the debate ends, and your opponent loses all momentum. That was a lesson Tobacco[1] took a bit too long to finally learn.

Sometimes your opponent is a customer (or client, for our purposes the two are interchangeable). And, as the adage goes, "The customer is always right." Of course, nothing could be further from the truth, but the customer *is* always the customer. As you will learn, some customers you have to keep, but some you can get rid of and make more money as a result.

You can also use psychology to get customers to buy more of your products including products that they originally never wanted to buy and, to be honest, don't need. I'll show you how. And, like the tobacco industry, it is all perfectly legal. If you bought this book to learn how to illegally make a huge profit, you will be disappointed.

But you will learn how the government and regulators can be your friends. No, that's wrong. They will not be your "friends," they will be your business partners and very good business partners at that. In fact, if you are lucky enough, smart enough, and savvy enough, you may get free loans from them and be able to open your own bank. What's more, they can do for you what

---

[1] Throughout the book, when "Tobacco" is capitalized it refers to the industry, otherwise, reference is to the plant.

you can't do for yourself: eliminate any advantage your competitors have and keep new players from entering your industry.

How's this for a promise? I'll show you how, by having your taxes *raised* and your number of customers *lowered*, you will make *more* money. And, by the way, if I were a betting man, I would bet that you are not charging your clients enough.

Then there are your employees to consider. You can't run your business without them. If the tobacco industry does not have the lowest turnover rate of any industry, then they are mighty close to the top of the list. What's more, they have a totally volunteer salesforce. I'm going to tell you the secret of how they achieved both.

I'm also going to tell you the two things that can save your company, or at least save you, a lot of money. Like most things, they are pretty simple and straightforward, such as having a lawyer keeping you on the straight and narrow and out of court, and a calendar so you never forget that which, if forgotten, could cost you your business.

Heaven knows that business owners, in today's day and age, with cybersecurity, employee social media behavior, government regulation, the media, and whatever surprise is waiting around the corner, have to deal with a lot of stress. I will provide you with somewhat of a guide to reduce or eliminate stress while taking control of your company's risk management strategies.

Of course, everyone will agree that stress reduction is good for your health. So, ironically, learning from the tobacco industry, as opposed to using their products, can be good for your personal health, not to mention your corporate wellbeing.

Ready? Let's get started.

INTRODUCTION: SMOKING KILLS

Debunking common misconceptions is a popular pastime. Someone says something, it sounds logical, others repeat it, it becomes a meme, and before you know it, everyone believes it. But just because "everyone believes it" does not make it true. Impression may be reality, but reality is not necessarily fact.

Surprisingly, or perhaps not so surprisingly, most are not all that important. For example, I know you probably want to believe it but, no, the Great Wall of China, despite what you may have heard, cannot be seen from outer space.

Allow me to ruin some of your other beliefs: Lightening can strike twice in the same place. If you swallow gum, it will not take seven years to digest. Sorry, but despite what your mother told you, there is no scientific basis to the warning that you must wait half an hour after eating before swimming.

And, sadly, according to his granddaughter, Dean Martin was not a heavy drinker. It was all an act. But it was a good act and anyone lucky enough to watch an appearance of his on *The Tonight Show Starring Johnny Carson*, should get a kick out of it. (You can find them on YouTube.) But that's a good kick, not a kick in the gut. That type of kick is when you hear about the ramifications of smoking on the public purse. Allow me to explain:

It is arguably false that smokers cost the taxpayer more than non-smokers in their lifetime. Although taxes and public services vary widely by country and jurisdiction, in many parts of the world it is simply not true. What is true is that many, many smokers contract a disease related to smoking and it is that disease, that illness, that costs the system. The problem is that that negates the fact that, like everyone else, all smokers are eventually going to die, but they may die of something that has nothing to do with smoking. Here's the salient point:

Most countries run public healthcare systems. (Despite popular opinion to the contrary, the US system is the largest.) According to research by Dr. Doll, who we shall meet shortly, on average smoking costs a smoker eleven years of their life. In other words, they will die eleven years sooner than if they had not smoked. Government old-age benefit programs are, sorry to have to tell you this, legal Ponzi schemes. It can be safely argued that people utilize these programs, i.e., they cost the government the most during the last third of their lives. That's when they retire and most benefits kick in.

Now, the smoker's healthcare needs, when they are dying, are costing the healthcare system money. There's no debating that. But, by dying 11 years earlier than they would have had they not smoked, they are also not collecting 11 years of Social Security/old-age benefits. So, in a sick way (pun intended), smokers are doing society a financial favor by smoking because literally, at the end of the day, they are costing the government, the country, less than their non-smoking fellow citizens.

Do not misunderstand me. Smoking is a disgusting habit. It is dangerous. It kills. You should not do it. I am against smoking tobacco. But the fact that it does not constitute a national financial burden in the way that most people believe it does, does not detract from my just expressed thoughts and warnings. Knowing the truth is never a bad thing. It's a positive. And, sometimes, it's shocking.

The mantra, "If we raise taxes fewer people will smoke," is also not true. It's a myth. People are addicted to nicotine, a substance, by the way, that is naturally found in the tobacco plant. If they need to smoke, they will find a way. That "way," is the black market. Instead of buying their smokes at the corner store, and paying taxes, they will buy them from the guy on the corner with the gym bag. You know, the guy who does not charge taxes because he doesn't pay them, not to mention duties. So, the smoker still smokes, he just buys his, or her, smokes illegally. The seller makes money, the government loses money. Since cigarette revenues drop, the government declares a "win," claiming that fewer people are smoking. But the reality is the opposite.

What's more, these illegal sales are normally not done by the pack, but by the carton. The product may be contraband or counterfeit. So, in addition to the threat from tar and nicotine, who knows what is really in these cigarettes? Moreover, the sellers are not checking IDs and may very well be selling to minors.

The tobacco industry surely knows this. Some companies have been known to conduct what are called "pack swap surveys." They pick up garbage at festivals and sporting events and their representatives go around and offer people a fresh pack of cigarettes in exchange for their packs, regardless of how many cigarettes are in the pack. Most people think this is the tobacco companies' way of getting people to change brands. There is probably truth to that, but more importantly, they are analyzing the packs they receive to determine the number of illegal packs consumed in a particular location.

So, as taxes rise, government revenues decline, the prevalence of smoking has decreased, but the number of smokers has steadily increased, at least this has been the case since about 1990 when the number rose to about 1.1 billion. This shows that increasing taxes to decrease the number of smokers may not work, and that the anti-smoking campaigns have not entirely succeeded in stopping younger people from starting to smoke. Since there are more people in the world today than three decades ago, the actual number of smokers is rising despite the decrease in the prevalence of the habit.

CONTENTIOUS COUNSEL

Another myth is that the tobacco companies spike nicotine in tobacco products to raise the potency of the product to increase addiction. The opposite is true. The actual process of manufacturing cigarettes lowers the amount of nicotine in the finished product. Frankly, the amount of tar, nicotine and carbon monoxide contained within cigarettes has to comply with International Standards Organization (ISO) and, in the US, FTC regulations. To lower the amount of nicotine and tar, the cigarette manufacturers place filters on the cigarettes and make laser perforations, so the cigarettes burn quicker, and the smoker inhales less toxins. There is no manipulation to make the cigarette more addictive, at least to my knowledge.

The only analogy I can offer may be the addiction of millions to caffeine. How many people can't start their day without their first cup of coffee? How many go through actual withdrawal and get violent headaches when they are not able to get their caffeine fix? It's a vice, albeit pleasurable and not deadly, but a vice, an addiction, nonetheless.

Now for the important misconception, marketing to children. Up until the 1960s, cigarettes were marketed to everyone; there were few age restrictions on smoking. There was no focused campaign directed specifically at children. It is simply false to make the charge. Even though it will spoil the chronology, let me once and for all put to rest the issue of trying to get children addicted to cigarettes.

The first claim that is made is that the manufacturers added tasty flavors to cigarettes, such as fruit and other sweets, to get children to smoke. Adults like those flavors as much as children. They have ever since they were young! Liquor now comes flavored, such as fruit flavored vodka.

I am a fan of Major League Baseball. In the ninth inning of a 2023 season game, I noticed that the advertisement behind Homeplate, the prime real estate at Rogers Centre in Toronto (because the camera is always on it), was for Mike's Hard Iced Tea, with their slogan emphasized in large lettering, "Bringing the Lemon to Hard Iced Tea." Does anyone honestly believe that the Blue Jays or Major League Baseball is trying to entice children, of which there were many in the stadium, to drink alcoholic beverages? Of course not. Adults like the taste of lemons. They are marketing to adults, not children.

And then there are the cartoon characters. Well, Joe Camel was not meant for children. The entire Camel family were adult camels. Manufacturers used cartoon characters because they did not want to have to deal with, pay, talent (actors). And what of the Budweiser frogs? No one claimed Bud was trying to get children to drink. Just because something appeals to children does not mean it is meant for children.

If you originally met the Flintstones when the show was first broadcast, it was not on the Saturday morning cartoons. Fred and Barney advertised Winston cigarettes. But at the time, the cartoon was shown on prime time, and was meant for adult audiences. The show actually dealt with adult issues. Albeit a cartoon, *The Flintstones* was the first television show to depict a husband and wife, wait for it, sleeping in the same bed. *South Park* was not the first adult cartoon on television.

Back in the day, everyone was the focus of tobacco marketing campaigns because everyone could legally smoke. Physicians even prescribed cigarettes because it was believed that nicotine could help with medical conditions: sooth anxiety, promote weight-loss, even help with depression. These were not carnival charlatans but real, honest to goodness, licensed physicians.

Now let's be fair. Don't judge those medical practitioners by today's standards. They did not have the information then that we have now. They honestly thought they were helping their patients.

It was part of the culture. Growing up, and this was far from unique, my parents were smokers. (I started when I was 15 and continued for the next 21 years.) My father was a cigar and pipe smoker. He had a smoking room in the house. My mother smoked French cigarettes. Many people smoked in the 1970s and 1980s. Most thought nothing of it from a health perspective. It was a societal norm that overrode the growing health consciousness. It took decades for the anti-smoking sentiment to sweep over North America. Accordingly, throughout my childhood many,

many people smoked, and it was socially acceptable. In fact, at dinner parties, along with presenting guests with coffee and chocolates, a tray of cigarettes was often available.

In fact, also on that tray, or perhaps on a tabletop, could have been a work of art created by the hosts' children. It was common, acceptable and, to a degree, expected, that one of the projects children would have in school (Arts and Crafts) and definitely at summer camp, was to make an ashtray for Mom or Dad, which they would proudly display at home or the office. It was a different time, to say the least.

Think about those old black and white movies. Someone gets sick, someone has been shot, and what does the friendly old town doc give his patient? A cigarette. It wasn't a product placement; it was a medical treatment to make the person feel better. It worked (supposedly) in real life, so why not in the movies?

Destroying any semblance of a chronology, when I eventually left Tobacco and moved to Toronto, I was surprised to discover just how deeply rooted the anti-smoking sentiment was in Canadian and American society. That was not the case in Europe. Tobacco was not as vilified abroad. In North America, the ideas that were fairly, to use a current word, "woke" and misinformed, were considered fact, no matter how ridiculous.

People honestly believed: Every time you smoke a cigarette your lungs bleed for 25 seconds. Tobacco companies intentionally spike cigarettes with nicotine to get people addicted. They are giving children free cigarettes to get them addicted.

In Toronto, at cocktail parties, I would refrain from mentioning that I came from Tobacco not because I did not want to be the center of conversation, as had been the case in Europe where people were honestly interested in the business, the industry. I simply did not want to have to spend the evening fruitlessly debating with people who simply did not have the facts.

To return to our chronology:

Back in 1964 things started to change in the United States, which eventually had a ripple effect on the rest of the world, because the health impacts of Tobacco products became more widely known. Yet, tobacco is still here today.

Why? How? These are the questions I will answer in the following pages. There is nothing wrong with learning from the tobacco industry. Many of you already have. Many of you have businesses that are successful because, albeit unknowingly, you have already copied at least one very important lesson from Tobacco.

CHAPTER 1:
YOU'VE COME A LONG WAY BABY

Cigarette manufacturing was automated in 1881. While Henry Ford may have come up with the assembly line, Tobacco came up with automation. A machine was created that could produce 200 cigarettes in one minute. Previously, it took 50 workers to accomplish that feat.

Think about it. Automation makes production quicker. It makes production more efficient. One machine does the work of 50 people.

But wait. The result of the automation of cigarette manufacturing was that while the retail price was cut by half, production rose from 500 million units a year to 10 billion by 1910. No one lost their job. Jobs were created.

Seventy-five percent market share is every business owner's dream. So is having 75% of your product sold to one client, who is not going to go away for the foreseeable future and, even if they do, it does not matter because they are giving your product away, for free, to their millions of employees who will continue to use your product long after the client stops buying from you and stops giving your product to their employees for free. Sounds pretty good, doesn't it? But then...

By 1944, 400 billion cigarettes were being manufactured annually in the United States. As noted, about 75% were sold to one client. That client was a little thing called the United States Government or, to be more specific, the War Department (aka the Department of Defense or Pentagon). Soldiers, sailors, marines, and airmen received the cigs along with their C-rations, helping to make fighting a world war a little less unpleasant. And, as noted, they got them for free. The federal government was the largest consumer and distributor of cigarettes. It was Washington that addicted the nation to tobacco. Today, the Federal Drug Administration (FDA) regulates the product in the USA. So, they are culpable. If tobacco is so bad, they could have, should have, and would have gotten rid of it, unless, of course, they had an ulterior motive in keeping the industry alive and well. (This will be a theme to which we will return.)

Now let's be honest, every business wants their product to be addictive. Are we not addicted to our smart phones? How often do you check to see if you have e-mails or social media messages? Not to be crude, but what do you do first thing in the morning, check your phone, or go to the bathroom?

Nothing wrong with smart phones, you say. We all know that people, mainly children, can't seem to get away from social media. How do they access it? Their phones. Most parents just thought it was a silly waste of time. "Go out! Get some sun! Read a book!" Yet we now know that, allegedly (While I no longer practice law, I am still a lawyer by profession.) the social media giants, and especially Facebook, knew that social media addiction was dangerous.

Tobacco is legal. Social media is legal. Both are regulated. I'll get into Tobacco presently. But let's just consider social media. As noted, the tool for social media is, mainly, the cell phone. Cell phone use is regulated. You can't hold a phone, let alone text, and drive. In some places you can't text and walk on the streets! This is government regulation of perfectly legal activities. Why? The excuse is "public health" or "public safety." We'll get back to that as well.

My point is that there are many legal products that have been, and are, regulated. But only one industry has reached the heights (or, if you prefer, the depths) of Tobacco. We need to learn how this happened so we can benefit from the good and avoid the bad.

But first we need a history lesson:

As I already explained, once upon a time doctors used to prescribe cigarettes. Not only that, back in the '50s and '60s they would smoke while seeing patients. One doctor who especially liked to smoke was Richard Doll who I mentioned earlier.

Dr. Doll proudly served as an officer in the British Armed Forces during World War Two, and was a committed smoker. After the War, he became one of the world's leading epidemiologists. He was the one who discovered that smoking was not the equivalent of a medical treatment but closer to a not-so-friendly game of Russian Roulette.

In 1949, working at the Medical Research Council with Dr. Bradford Hill, an epidemiologist at the London School of Hygiene, they started to investigate the spike in lung cancer rates in Great Britain in the first half of the twentieth century.

At first, they thought the culprit might be the tar that was being used to repair the country's war-damaged roads. Then they turned their attention to human-made environmental pollutants.

Their methodology was simple: They interviewed cancer patients about their family histories, diets, employment, and previous diseases. Then, when 647 out of 649 patients said they were smokers, the duo had their answer and Dr. Doll quit smoking.

Doll and Hill published their first report in 1951 to the consternation of their peers who did not want to give up their favorite vice. But the good doctors pushed forward in the face of adversity with Churchillian fortitude. So now, instead of interviewing cancer patients, they decided to interview British doctors who smoked.

In 1954 they published the results of their research in *The British Medical Journal*, confirming their previous conclusions. Of course, now their fellow physicians had to take note. Not only in Britain, but also around the world. In 1964, Dr. Luther Terry issued the *US. Surgeon*

CONTENTIOUS COUNSEL

General's Report which categorically linked tobacco consumption to a variety of serious illnesses. This may have been the end of tobacco as medicine, but it was the beginning of the beginning of Tobacco as a great business model in a cowardly (as opposed to brave) new world.

In an unprecedented step, health warnings began to appear on cigarette packages and advertisements in many countries around the world. (For perspective, it was only in 1968 that the Motion Picture Association of America started rating movies.)

The 1964 *Report* was an unprecedented publishing success. It has unwittingly become one of the most often-cited publications in the history of the printed word, even beating out the Bible. Every pack of cigarettes has a quote from the *Report*, a warning that what you were about to do could harm you.

Fast forward to 1998 and things really got interesting. No longer was the discussion about packaging. The attorneys general of 46 states had sued the four largest tobacco companies in the US. They arrived at what can only be described as an epic settlement, the Master Settlement Agreement or MSA. Why?

It was all due to a whistleblower by the name of Jeffrey Wigand who, in 1995, appeared on the TV show *Sixty Minutes*. He revealed that the tobacco companies knew about the dangers of their products long before Dr. Terry's 1964 *Report*. They knew nicotine was addictive and that tobacco was deadly. The MSA was the industry's attempt to avoid billions of dollars in lawsuits that would have crippled them.

Just as an aside, while virtually all cigarettes are manufactured by the companies that signed the MSA, there are a few smaller manufacturers who chose not to sign. Moreover, they are permitted to freely advertise their products (in the USA) albeit within certain limits. The catch is that the cigarettes are sold on Indigenous reservations and are arguably not the same quality as those sold by the national manufacturers. In some cases, they are sold neither in packs nor cartons; smokers purchase a clear plastic bag of 1,000 individual sticks. What is more, since they are purchased on the reservations, they are extremely inexpensive as they are not taxed or are only slightly taxed. In theory, they are not supposed to be used off the reservation, but the reality is the opposite. In any event, this amounts to such a miniscule amount of cigarette production that, basically, no one cares.

Returning to the MSA, it is important to ask, Why would the government want to settle? Well, for now, suffice to say tobacco was an important American crop, a lucrative source of tax revenue, a major US employer, and a product enjoyed by tens of millions of loyal customers, also known as voters.

The lawsuits in US courts, civil suits, with witnesses barely able to breath let alone speak, on the witness stand, saying that their condition was the fault of the bad men sitting "over there" in their $5,000 suits, was not something industry lawyers were looking forward to experiencing. And, if this actually happened, the final nail in Tobacco's coffin would be the "Failure to Warn" clause which means exactly what you think. They knew of the danger and did not tell anyone. Moreover, even today, let alone back then, if you look on a package of cigarettes you will see the warning, but you won't see any instructions. The company does not tell, and has never told, customers what their product is for or how to use it, but only what the consequences of its use could be. (Of course, they can't tell customers how to use their product safely, because it can't be used safely.) But again, smoking tobacco is 100% legal.

Because of Wigand, it was no longer even about "Failure to Warn" but rather "Withholding Pertinent Information." The industry's back was up against the wall and the firing squad was locked, loaded, and moving quickly from "Ready. Aim." to "Fire!"

Enter President William Jefferson Clinton. He did not want to be at the helm while a major US industry was destroyed. So, instead of destroying it, he regulated it. Which, ironically, meant that he partnered with Tobacco, as crazy as that may sound. (But, then again, we are talking about the president who "did not inhale.")

What was the MSA? It was the Deal of the Century. It was practically genius. It would not be an exaggeration to say that it was a legal miracle. It was the deal that saved the US tobacco industry from almost certain ruin. In exchange for a very large payout, as well as agreeing "voluntarily" to major concessions regarding the sale and marketing of their products, the industry was guaranteed immunity from all future state and federal lawsuits. It protected them more than any other amount of legal immunity would have done. They also agreed to shut down their lobbying efforts.

What did the government, meaning the Clinton Administration, get out of it? Well, since the MSA was an "agreement" and not a "law," there was no issue of restricting constitutional rights such as freedom of speech or expression. Also, while the government would be taking in revenue from the deal, technically, there were no new taxes. Let's explore this uniquely American solution to a government funding problem.

The money from the MSA comes from the tobacco companies who raise their prices to cover their commitment. In other words, consumers pay for the MSA. What, you ask, does the government do with the money? It goes to fund state healthcare and anti-smoking campaigns (or at least it should; in Alabama some historical MSA funding was used to build golf courses). In other words, the industry agreed to foot the bill for trying to convince consumers not to buy its products. The result, as we will see, was the exact opposite of what anyone with even a scintilla of common sense would have expected.

But enough history lesson for now. This is a business book, not a history text.

How the industry has been able to survive and prosper in the face of litigation and regulation is our focus. This is not a book about how to get away with selling a deadly product, that should not be sold in the market today and would not be except for historic reasons. It is just that there is so much to be learned from the experience of Tobacco that I believe it is a story which must be told.

For example, Tobacco launched one of the most successful marketing campaigns ever that was geared towards women. In the 1920s and '30s, smoking was not considered ladylike. After World War Two, that turned around and sales doubled because women started smoking. Women were purposely seen smoking as they walked down Fifth Avenue in Manhattan in the Easter Day Parade. Many of you are probably old enough to remember the 1970s' Virginia Slims, "You've come a long way baby," commercials and advertisements, the source of the title of this chapter. In fact, for women, it was almost as successful as the Marlboro Man was for advertising to men. (Speaking of Virginia Slims, their January 1, 1972 advertisement during the last half hour of that evening's *Tonight Show Starring Johnny Carson* was the final television advertisement to air for cigarettes in the United States.)

So, TV ads are gone. Also, most vending machines are gone. Something else I have yet to mention, it was agreed that ads could only be placed in magazines primarily aimed at persons over the minimum age to purchase cigarettes. So where did (and do) cigarette manufacturers advertise? In pornographic magazines, and similar publications aimed at an 18+ audience. After all, teenagers never look at porn, right?

What about the warnings on cigarette packages? Are they effective? In the US, the warning is simply written in a small font. In Canada and Europe, there is a picture of what a diseased organ looks like. This is not, "This is your brain; this is your brain on drugs" showing pretty eggs frying in a pan. These pictorial depictions are, to put it mildly, disgusting. And, to answer my previous question, yes, they are effective. True, today there are a billion smokers, more than ever. Yes, a billion smokers, more than ever, but the percentage of smokers has dropped.

Let's use Canada as the example since Canada is the world leader in the fight against smoking:

Health Canada's goal was to reduce the number of adult smokers. They instituted a full advertising ban. Education programs were launched to discourage smoking. Restrictions were placed on where products could be sold. Cigarettes could no longer be sold in drug stores or vending machines. They raised the legal smoking age. The price of a pack of smokes would rise once or twice a year. Descriptors such as Light, Mild, Ultra, as well as additives like menthol, were eliminated. Moreover, there were no more "points of sale;" cigarettes were literally hidden from view. No one knew which cigarettes were available. Nothing was at eye level.

Were all these restrictions effective? Thirty years ago, 25 to 30 percent of adults in Canada smoked. Today, it's 10 to 15 percent. So, yes, as a percentage of the population and in absolute numbers, there are fewer smokers in Canada. In fact, the industry may have lost half of its customers. Yet, despite the restrictions, the manufacture, distribution, and sale of cigarettes are still completely legal. And business? It has never been better. How is this possible?

Thirty years ago, a pack cost around one dollar. Today, over $15. Most of that is tax. In general, the manufacturer takes 15% of the total sale price meaning, their margins are nearly 10 times what they were 30 years ago. And then there is a game which is played. The government raises taxes once or twice a year. The government gets blamed for the price increase. The manufacturer adds one or two pennies on its own. Consumers neither know, realize, nor care. After all, it's only a couple of cents. And this is not new. In fact, speaking at an Imperial Conference on May 7, 1907, Winston Churchill remarked, "The imposition of such a small duty as a shilling on a commodity produced in such vast abundance as wheat, might quite easily be swamped or concealed by the operation of other more powerful factors." Swamping and concealing are exactly what the tobacco companies do, and no one blames them. All the blame for the increase in price falls on the government – federal, state, provincial, whatever. In other words, tobacco companies, despite everything, are now making ten times more per pack than they were thirty years ago, and no one blames them for the increase in cost.

And it's not just because of the "game" with the taxes. Since there is no advertising, all the money they used to spend on advertising and marketing now goes to their bottom line, with some notable exceptions which I will discuss. And the existing companies have no new competitors. There are also fewer brand varieties, two instead of eight, so that lowers costs. Since consumers literally can't see their products on the store shelves, there are no new entrants into the industry because they can't advertise so no one could ask for the product since they wouldn't know it exists. Market shares are basically fixed and completely protected from competition. It's perfect: Half the number of smokers makes the government happy; manufacturers are making 10 times the money so they're happy. It's a marriage made in heaven (or possibly hell?).

There are analogies in other industries.

Let's start with gasoline. I am writing as war rages between Ukraine and Russia, and the United States is imposing sanctions on the import of Russian petroleum and natural gas. The price for a gallon of gas is now well over $4.00. But only a small fraction of US gasoline comes from Russia. OPEC has only recently placed limits on their output. So why the price rise? Someone has to be making money off of a gallon of gas. And the government has definitely not raised taxes. So, the logical culprits are the petroleum companies, but President Biden blames Putin as well as the producers. Granted, he, Putin, appears to be the devil incarnate, but he does not appear to be responsible for the price of a gallon of gas in Dallas, Texas.

Don't like that analogy? How about the airline industry? An airline goes bankrupt. Competitors flying the same routes, raise their prices. Their expenses have not gone up, but market forces allow them to raise their prices. They can get away with it because it seems logical. Fewer providers mean less competition which means higher prices. And consumers literally buy that even though it is as silly as the cost of a flight on the day before Thanksgiving being significantly higher than the price a week before the holiday, even though the costs to the airline are the same. Consumers get taken advantage of because what they really buy into isn't a product but a common wisdom which is patently false.

In the United States there is a balance between legal protections and governmental restrictions. "Unalienable" rights are not unalienable if they can be restricted. So, citizens have freedom of speech and freedom of expression, but no cigarette ads on television and radio. Fact is that the idea that "the public health" overrides the Constitution has never been directly tested in the Supreme Court. So, apparently, it does. (The paradox of Big Tobacco is that their products can kill you, but using them is an adult choice. Some will say "yes," some "no.") And, while these bans are by law, all other bans on cigarette advertising, as we will see, are "voluntary." (For that matter, there are no gun advertisements other than product placements in movies, such as *Pulp Fiction*, for the AK-47. And to be fair, there were those cartons of Lucky Stripe and Pall Mall cigarettes that fell out of a truck in the opening scene of *Beverly Hills Cop*, which was definitely a product placement!)

The tobacco industry likely will be the litmus test for regulations in the future. Is it really a question of public health or not? What is to happen to fast food? Alcohol? Sugar? Cell phones? Pharmaceuticals? Electronics? And now, in light of the FTX disaster, bitcoin? Restrictions could be based on public safety but not always exclusively so. It may appear the government is trying to protect or save people from themselves but, as we have already seen, such things can be deceptive.

Again, tobacco is unique because when used as intended it is so potentially harmful. You may not know when it will harm you, but you know it will. And, because nicotine is a drug, the FDA regulates it. To be clear, nicotine is not what kills, it is what addicts. What kills is the combustion of the tobacco and its inhalation. In low amounts, nicotine is not harmful, *per se*. That is why nicotine patches are sold, along with gum. They are relatively safe, if used properly, and can actually be beneficial. And, as of yet, they are not regulated in the same way as cigarettes. So why does the FDA not just ban cigarettes which consist of tobacco which, albeit naturally, includes nicotine?

Smokers like to make parallels between smoking and drinking alcohol or eating fast food. Aren't they all bad for you? Can't they all kill you? Not true. No one knows when or if someone will get cancer or any of the other 250 deceases associated with smoking. Is it the first or the thousandth cigarette? Smoking causes cancer in some smokers but not all. Why? Scientific proof does not yet exist to prove what is the one factor that caused the cancer in one specific individual person. But alcohol and fast food, if used in moderation, can't hurt you. A 5:00 pm cocktail may keep you alive into your 90s. At least it will not guarantee to keep you from your tenth decade! One salt and fat inundated beef patty every now and again won't harm you unless you have a preexisting medical condition. But the same can be said of just about anything you ingest into your body, except cigarettes.

One final analogy which, I promise, I'll try to make as mildly disgusting as possible.

A new fat free oil was invented. Olestra was its name. Pringles used it. Life was finally worth living. You could eat as many Pringles as you wanted and not gain weight. Except for one little thing. (And here I must keep my promise.) Olestra had a rather severe intestinal side effect. So, the FDA banned it. Emphysema? OK. Diarrhea? No way!

Oh, and by the way, in April 2022 the FDA announced it was banning menthol (as had already been done in Canada and the UK) in all cigarettes and cigars. Not banning the nicotine that addicts, nor the tobacco that kills, but the menthol that provides the pleasant flavor. Apparently, the government doesn't mind if you kill yourself as long as you don't have a pleasant taste in your mouth when you're doing it.

How many people die each year from smoking? In 2019, 7.7 million people (which roughly translates to the population of Dallas, Texas) died from smoking. That's 21,095 people per day, worldwide. How many people died from eating Pringles? None. So why the FDA's decision? The government makes billions of dollars from the sale of cigarettes but only state sales tax from the sale of a tube of Pringles.

And it is not just the US. In the UK, if the chancellor of the exchequer were to ban the sale of cigarettes, in order to recoup the money lost, they would have to raise every taxpayer's personal income tax by something close to 11%. Not bloody likely, mate.

You think smokers are addicted to tobacco? The real addict is the government to all that beautiful tax revenue. The government is the best business partner anyone could have.

Do you think things are changing? You are wrong. History is repeating itself.

The British Government is now doing the same thing with vaping that was done with cigarettes. Smoking is an epidemic and a tragedy. Vaping is less bad and a way to wean people off cigarettes. So, His Majesty's Government is giving away free vapes, to get rid of cigarettes and then, when they declare success, they'll get rid of vapes.

So, tobacco products are heavily taxed. In the US there are sales taxes, excise tax, tobacco duties - a percentage or fixed amount per pack – and the MSA payment, which can be a fixed amount. There may also be a tariff on imported brands of cigarettes and on domestic brands if the tobacco in them is imported. All of these taxes can determine the base price of cigarettes to which the manufacturer adds their costs. This is not unique to the US; in Italy and many other countries, the government sets the price.

Again, I am not going to advise you how to sell a dangerous product. I want to teach you how companies have been able to survive and prosper in the face of litigation, regulation, and legislation that many thought would cripple the industry. That is the wisdom of how to survive and thrive when faced with combative elements coming against you – public opinion, lawsuits, government regulation and legislation, the medical community, interest groups – throwing everything at you. It is what, under normal circumstances, is called "business continuity."

Now I know I said that this is a business book. And, hopefully, you have already learned a great deal about the business of Tobacco. But part of business is morality, which is subjective at best. There are some things all people agree on and anyone who disagrees would rightly be ostracized. Best example, abuse. No one condones the abuse of a child. That is our universal morality.

But before moving on to the more traditional business aspects of Tobacco, it is important that we consider the philosophical. We already touched on it: The MSA, as an agreement and not law, means that there is no contradiction, legally speaking, between the rights of an American to freedom of speech and expression, and the denial of the rights of tobacco companies to market their products. Of course, that's rubbish. The contradiction exists; it is simply ignored by universal consent. The ends, in this case, justify the means.

And if you like tobacco, just wait till you realize what is around the corner. But I must first, once again, don my lawyer's cap. Just to be clear, this chapter is a philosophical discussion of the topic. It is not medical advice in any way, shape, or form. I am neither a medical professional nor a scientist.

Don't like the fact that tobacco is legal? While not everyone is in favor of the legalization of cannabis or psilocybin, the natural compound found in Magic Mushrooms that gets users "high," as you probably know, marijuana is now legal in Canada and numerous states in the US. But did you know that British Columbia and Oregon have legalized some forms of psychedelics for research and medicinal purposes? "The times," as Bob Dylan used to sing, "they are a changin'."

The issue here is not about getting stoned. It is about recognizing the sovereignty of adult human beings to make decisions over their bodies, health, and consciousness, while doing no harm to others. I fully recognize that a case can be made that indirectly and unintentionally smoking marijuana can harm others, akin to second-hand smoke. That is a sociological discussion, and, with your permission, I want to remain in the realm of the philosophical. Usually, such impact on others can simply be dealt with by not allowing the activity in public places. If the person using, is alone, they are only impacting themselves.

Here, for me, it the moral/philosophical issue: If you are in Canada, the United States or Britain, or for that matter in most, if not all, other countries, you live in a country where sovereignty over your body and consciousness are not usually recognized. That means you, we, are not living in a "free society" in any meaningful sense of the term. We live in a hypocritical society where abortion restrictions, mandatory vaccinations, and the control of alcohol and pharmaceuticals is imposed on society. (For the record, I am not "anti-vax.")

But our governments are not against altered states of consciousness. In fact, they support industries which enable individuals to achieve such states. The US, Canadian and British governments all allow Big Pharma to make billions from drugs that alter states of consciousness, such as anti-depressants, which have been called horrible drugs, potentially harmful, but, as long as you have a doctor's prescription, they are perfectly legal to use. And, of course, alcohol also changes one's state of consciousness, is very harmful to the user, extremely dangerous, but is totally legal.

Society, it seems, is only against particular kinds of altered states of consciousness. It's a mixed bag which appears not to have any rhyme or reason. Yet we, as a society, do not generally question the existing system of governmental control which regulates mind-altering substances.

There does not appear to be any logical process by which the government chooses which drugs, or vices, are legal and which are not. But appearances can be deceiving. In this case, the common denominator seems to be money. If a product becomes essential to the government making money (read: taxes), as with tobacco, it will not be made illegal and will not be forced to be withdrawn from the market. It will be regulated. It may be placed behind the counter. But it will be available to consumers.

Times can change. Cannabis was illegal, now, not so much. Before the 1970s, psilocybin was legal. Until recently, as noted, it has been banned but, just as cannabis slowly became legal, so now will psilocybin. Will it be sold legally throughout the US and Canada in a year? A decade? Who knows.

Nothing is ever totally new. Coke, as everyone knows, is called "coke" because it used to contain cocaine and other barbiturates. It was not meant to be a cold drink on a hot day, but a tonic that would literally cure what ailed you. Then the government forced Coke to change its recipe. And, of course, back then the government had nothing to lose. It didn't make any money off of Coke or its ingredients.

If the government does not have any particular values, or standards, for determining what is permitted and what is not, then it is not about keeping individuals or society safe, but about the government making money. If you can ensure that your product will earn money for the people, i.e., the government, who control your industry, they will not only allow you to operate but will protect your product from being outlawed.

Let me turn to a totally unrelated example: electric vehicles.

EVs are good for the environment. They help combat climate change. They are the panacea for saving the planet. They eliminate the need for fossil fuels. Well, not exactly.

First, a percentage, it varies depending on where you live, of that "clean" electricity which you are using to charge your EV, comes from fossil fuels. Second, let's say it only costs you $5 to charge your vehicle at home. Even if it costs twice or three times that amount to charge at a commercial site, it is still a lot cheaper than filling up a tank with gas. So, what could possibly be the problem?

The government supports the EV industry. One day, it is safe to assume, there will be more EVs than gas-powered vehicles. That's a good thing. But as fewer and fewer people fill up at the pump, the government will earn less and less tax revenue. Don't bother looking; you will not find one. There is no example of the government losing tax revenue and simply walking away. They have to make up for the loss. How will they do that in the case of lost gas tax revenue? Perhaps a mileage tax? Perhaps increasing the tax on electricity? Carbon in the atmosphere goes down and your electric bill goes up.

And don't kid yourself. Just as tobacco tax revenue goes for a lot more than just supporting the healthcare system, gas tax revenue goes for a lot more than infrastructure – roads, tunnels, and bridges. Although there is a difference. Fewer smokers mean less of a burden on the healthcare network, but more EVs makes no difference at all on the impact on infrastructure (although, with less or no exhaust from vehicles, roads and bridges won't have to be cleaned as often). So, while the fossil fuel industry will lose most of its government protection (not all because fossil fuels are used for more than just automobile fuel), the EV industry will gain that protection because, for all intents and purposes, the government is the one creating the industry. Just like Tobacco, alcohol and pharma, EV has nothing to worry about, as long as it helps the government pay its bills.

Let's return to cannabis.

Despite what you may think, cannabis does not necessarily make you high. There are active components in cannabis, with THC and CBD being the two most commonly known. THC makes you high, alters your state of consciousness, and is incredibly good for pain relief. CBD, on the other hand, does not make you high as it has no psychoactive properties, helps with pain and inflammation, and has other health benefits. CBD, derived from hemp, is legal in the US and Canada, but is still illegal in many other countries.

Why is cannabis legal? It is a great revenue generator. In Canada, the federal government under Justin Trudeau controls the industry. Just as with tobacco and alcohol, taxes must be paid on "weed." The sale is regulated by the provinces through the granting of licenses. So, again, it's all about money. It is not about health. It is not about safety. To be kind, it is an example of unexpected consequences.

In my opinion, the government made two mistakes when legalizing marijuana, the consequences of which may not be known for decades. (In business, the "law of unintended consequences" should never be ignored.)

There are two primary ways to ingest marijuana, you can smoke it or eat (or drink) it. The preferred method is smoking. The user takes a bud, rolls it in paper, and lights it up. Inhalation of smoke containing THC is the quickest way to get high. Eating or drinking marijuana, as a drink, gummy or brownie, is a different experience because, while the user will still get high, it will take longer and may be less intense. Eating it can also upset some users' stomachs.

Nicotine is the tobacco equivalent of THC. A user can get their nicotine hit by using a patch, chewing gum, or eating a candy. There is no health downside to this because, as previously noted, while nicotine is addictive, in low doses, it is not bad for you. The bad part of smoking is the inhalation of the tar, carbon monoxide and other particles found in the actual smoke.

Eating cannabis is akin to eating nicotine. Smoking it is the same, only more so. The danger is in inhaling the smoke, just like with a regular cigarette. The problem is, one joint is equivalent to smoking about 20 Marlboros, a pack of cigarettes. Cigarettes have filters, are regulated, burn quicker and the tobacco is properly treated. However, only the sale of cannabis leaf is regulated, not the toxic constituents ingested in the use of the product itself.

That was the government's first mistake, not regulating the manufacture of marijuana cigarettes, or more importantly, not differentiating between ingestion methods. The second, which they also should have seen coming based on the Tobacco experience, was their inadvertent support for drug dealers. (As a general rule of thumb, making life easier for drug dealers is never a good thing.)

When you legalize something, you have to allow people to possess their purchases. Laws against possession of marijuana had to be amended. A person had to have the right to possess a quantity of product for their personal use. Being caught by the police with marijuana for personal use could no longer be a crime.

For sake of argument, since it depends on the jurisdiction, let's say the government permits an individual to have on their person 10 grams (.35 ounces) of marijuana. That does not appear to be a lot, but it actually is enough for 100 joints. So now a drug dealer, standing on a street corner, can have 100 joints on him (or her) and the police can't do a thing about it, unless they catch them in the act of selling the joints. That's still illegal.

Now why would someone buy a joint from some shady character on a street corner? For the same exact reason that they would buy a cigarette from them. When someone legally sells marijuana, they charge taxes. The dealer does not. The dealer undercuts the government price. Customers don't think about the quality of the product, just what they will have to pay.

And, for the record, in the fight against legal and illegal marijuana, even when marijuana has been made legal, as in California and New York, the illegal black market is still beating the legal market! Simply put, the black market undermines the legal market, by charging less. Customers don't care.

That's two very costly, and dangerous, mistakes the government made, especially when the threat of fentanyl is added to the equation.

My goal is to show the problems that can arise when similar industries, in this case those dealing with products that alter states of consciousness, are not uniformly regulated. Which is further proof, a subject I will delve into more deeply in Chapter 6, that regulation is good and can keep you in business – especially if the government prioritizes tax revenue over the health and safety of the individual. And shame on them!

And shame on you as a business owner if you make like an ostrich and bury your head in the sand instead of tackling problems head on, adapting your business model, plans and operational playbook to the new reality you are facing, instead of fighting it, because you will ultimately be more successful and keep your industry moving forward if you simply accept regulations. If Tobacco had not adapted to their new reality but had chosen to fight to the end, they would have probably lost. They listened and they thrived, which is what every business wants.

How do I know this is accurate? Well, before I entered the industry, the policy was to deny that nicotine was addictive and that smoking kills. That was not playing well in Washington and many other political capitals, and the industry was suffering. Once the policy was simplified, because there is nothing simpler than to just tell the truth, Tobacco was able to turn themselves around and succeed. (Just so you know, in all my years in Tobacco, I never sat in a meeting or heard anyone deny the truth about the dangers of our products which, I hasten to add, once again, are perfectly legal.)

So now let's get to the lessons businesses can learn based on my experience. But, to reiterate, this is not about clandestine transactions for which Tobacco is famous but which, in most cases, never happened; it is not about teaching how to circumvent the law; this is about teaching how not only to survive but to thrive while dealing with regulation, legislation, and pressure. I am not pro tobacco. I am pro learning from the experiences of the tobacco industry.

Today, as I write these words, companies are having to cope with "woke" culture. Proponents of "woke" want to place restrictions on what can be said and what can be done. They could very well succeed, resulting in restrictions and regulations on legal products and services akin to tobacco, like sugar, cell phones, and narcotics. Add to all of this global warming/climate change and the "green" agenda, not to mention COVID related restrictions, and a lot can be learned from the experiences of Big Tobacco.

I started my career at a time of immense change, much like we are witnessing today, at the end of the good ole days of sports sponsorships and huge marketing campaigns. My industry needed to change. So will yours. I witnessed that successful change (keep in mind, 60 years after the Surgeon General's *Report*, they are still in business, tobacco is still legal, and the industry is not only very profitable, but there are more smokers in the world today than ever before) and I look forward to witnessing your successful change too.

Ignore my advice at your own risk. Others have. As you no doubt know, there is a legislative process for the creation of new laws and regulations. There is always a consultation period. Legislators hear from the relevant industry about the financial, retail, social, and employment impact of the proposed new legislation. When I was in the hot seat, I reached out to my counterparts in, for example, the spirits (alcohol) industry. I asked them to join us in protesting proposed advertising restrictions on tobacco. They declined. They preferred to keep as low a profile as possible (probably because they didn't want to become associated with Big Tobacco). Now the government is going after them. If only they had listened...

SOURCES:

Churchill's remarks:
Liberalism and Socialism (1909: Rosetta Books, e-book edition, Loc. 871)

California and New York Cannabis laws:
https://www.politico.com/news/2022/11/13/california-black-market-weed-new-york-00066470

CHAPTER 2:
STEALING THE PLAYBOOK

Not all playbooks are secret and confidential. Tobacco's certainly isn't. And because Tobacco has been so successful, it is only natural for other industries to want to emulate it. But that is not something that I recommend. Thus, the impetus for writing this chapter.

It is my belief that the food industry has done too good a job learning from Tobacco. Originally, I wanted to draw a parallel between the addictive nature of nicotine and that of sugar, and the harmfulness of the ingredients in our favorite snacks with the dangers of inhaling smoke. It was clear to me that the lessons from Tobacco, taken by the food industry, have had a profound impact on the obesity epidemic in Canada, the US and the UK.

As I was writing this chapter, I learned I was not the first to draw the connection. I discovered a 2014 article by Dr. Cheryl Perry, Ph.D., and MeLissa Creamer, MPH, titled "The Childhood Obesity Epidemic: Lessons Learned from Tobacco," published in *The Journal of Pediatrics*.

(For the record, references to food and obesity in this chapter refer to their article.)

We have already seen how the US government addicted American GIs to cigarettes by giving them away with their C-rations. Prior to the 1964 Surgeon General's *Report*, the industry spent hundreds of millions of dollars marketing cigarettes to children. A 2012 report stated that, "Advertising and promotional activities by tobacco companies have shown to cause the onset and continuation of smoking among adolescents and young adults". Of course, this comment is historical in nature as all advertising stopped in 1998 as a result of the MSA. But the point is still valid. Advertise to adolescents and young adults, and you will have customers for life. How long that life will be is another matter...

Historically, cigarettes were cheap, and the industry suppressed health information that would have caused any rational person to avoid the sticks of death, if I may call them that. In other words, entice young people to use your products, keep them cheap and deny (read: lie) any negative health consequences and you have the outline of the old Tobacco playbook. Now we come to obesity.

First, it is not surprising that the food industry would want to learn from Tobacco. It is not an exaggeration to say, they are one and the same. Nabisco Brands was owned by R.J. Reynolds and Kraft foods was part of Philip Morris. (For the record, Kraft is the largest food manufacturer, and Philip Morris is the largest cigarette manufacturer, in the United States.)

Just as the odds of getting cancer are likely increased proportionally to the number of cigarettes one smokes, so too are the odds increased of becoming obese by the number of calories one ingests. Add to that the fact that unhealthy foods are readily available and inexpensive, and that most Americans lead "sedentary lifestyles," and you have a recipe for illness, first and foremost, diabetes and heart problems.

Surprisingly, in 1961, the US trailed behind such countries as Australia, Denmark, Germany, Norway, the UK, and even the USSR with a daily average of 2,900 calories consumed per person. By 2009 the US led the world with 3,700 calories per person per day. But there are calories, and then there are calories. Vegetable oils and sweeteners led the race for US caloric supremacy.

Lifestyle had as much to do with the increase in calories as anything else. Americans demanded food that required "little to no cooking, are convenient, do not spoil quickly and satisfy taste requirements." Of the 21,500 new foods introduced into the US market in 2010, almost half were candy, gum, snacks, or beverages, "all likely to be high in sugar and/or fat content". High fructose corn syrup accounts for over half of all sweeteners.

And then there are the hydrogenated oils which provide higher trans fatty acids, but increase shelf life. Who are the primary consumers, as in eaters, of these foods? Children and youth. Just as Tobacco knew that their future depended on getting people to start smoking early, so does the food industry. The difference, advertising by the former was outlawed, by the latter is legal.

A decade ago, children between the ages of two and 11, and adolescents between 12 and 17, would see, respectively, 13 and 16 ads a day for food, practically all of which had high amounts of sugar, fat, and salt. The ads worked. What the children saw was what they asked their parents to purchase. The result, adiposity, which is a fancy word for obesity, in children and youth.

The Children's Food and Beverage Advertising Initiative (CFBAI) was formed in 2006, by the Council for Better Business Bureaus. They wanted self-regulation of the food industry when it came to marketing to children. They had some success. Except for dairy products, marketing to children did drop $400 million between 2006 and 2009, but overall, advertising budgets remained constant.

That said, the fewer dollars were being spent more efficiently. For example, Internet marketing is replacing television ads. Moreover, while Tobacco first used *The Flintstones* to sell their wares, the food industry is securing marketing rights to characters from popular children's movies so that they can use them to adorn their packaging. It is as though the latest Disney character is endorsing the fatty salted cereal in the box that children are salivating for their parents to buy. This does not just include only packaged foods on supermarket shelves, but also the products sold at fast food restaurants. Think of the toys in a McDonald's "Happy Meal." Who, in the long-term, is exactly getting "happy?" McDonald's shareholders.

So, advertising of food goes to the targeted consumers while the price of food goes to their wallets. Food in the US is cheap in more ways than one. Not only is much of it bad for you, but it is inexpensive. That is intentional. The federal government does not want to ever have a repeat of the food lines and soup kitchens of the Great Depression. (US politicians cringe when recalling the lines of cars with drivers waiting to get food packages due to COVID lockdowns.) That means the food supply has to be ample and inexpensive. Corn, wheat (and cotton) were first subsidized in 1933. Price supports for tobacco, which made it possible for farmers to grow food crops which seasonally would fail, were in effect from 1938 to 2004. The Food Stamp Act of 1964 has given support to low-income families so they can buy food.

This, of course, is all good, except for one problem. For example, in the case of corn, it became such a cash crop that it was used for other purposes, such as ethanol. Well, if corn is going into a car's gas tank, it's not going into the driver's stomach, meaning there is less corn available for food and, therefore, the price of food rises. That is why there are now annual subsidies, to the tune of $10 billion a year, for corn, wheat, and soybeans.

Moreover, these cheap crops have meant the development of new, inexpensive foods, targeting the poor. The food is high in fat and sugar resulting in a disproportionate number of people with diabetes in certain demographics.

Just as the government protects Tobacco, the government protects farmers and by doing so, guarantees us access to those goodies that are far from good for us.

Finally, there is that little matter of inconvenient truth. Instead of listening to their mothers, the food industry listened to Tobacco and lied.

The CFBAI may be an acronym for a long name, but it has a short membership list. Its goal, self-regulation of advertising to children, may sound laudable but given that the members represent almost three-quarters of all food manufacturers, their motives should be suspect.

What most people don't realize is that only a small number of companies control the manufacture of food in the US. Four companies raise 60% of chickens. Consider the chicken feed (wheat and corn) used, its impact on cattle, and, of course, human consumption, and you can begin to appreciate the magnitude of the problem.

The food industry has to deal with food safety (mad cow disease and salmonella come to mind) and health related data showing a link between some foods and cancer, heart disease, or both.

Taking a page out of the Tobacco playbook (i.e., "Smoking does not cause cancer,") the food industry denied claims that there was a relationship between trans fats and disease. From the 1990s, that claim was repudiated. In 2003, the FDA required trans fat labeling on all packaged goods as of 2006. Some cities, including New York and Boston, banned trans fats from restaurants. ("No smoking on these premises!")

In both cases, the tobacco and food industries denied the dangers of their products until the evidence was overwhelming. Moreover, they refused to take any actions limiting sales until forced to by legislation. While the food industry is protected to a great degree by the government, people have to eat and farmers have to make a profit, repeating Tobacco's mistakes could cause the food industry to face limitations, for example, on advertising. But unlike cigarettes, a McDonald's franchise can't be hidden behind a counter the way a package of Marlboro's can!

Food shares three similarities with Tobacco: affordability, acceptability and availability. They will be the focus of the Conclusions to our journey through the Land of Tobacco. But for now, let's consider probably the most amazing anomaly found in this book: The fewer customers you have, the more money you'll earn.

SOURCE

Price support for Tobacco:
https://www.irs.gov/pub/irs-utl/farmers_atg_chapter_10.pdf

CHAPTER 3:
FEWER CUSTOMERS, MORE PROFIT

When we started this journey through what I hope you are finding to be the intriguing world of Big Tobacco, I tried to dispel some common wisdoms in an effort to show that things are not always what we believe them to be. People can say as many times as they want that tobacco companies try to addict children to their products, but it is simply not true. Perception is not always reality.

And neither is logic. It is perfectly logical to assume that an industry which is bleeding customers is also bleeding cash. What could be more logical? If you lose half your customers your revenue should decline proportionately. Your business should collapse. Your industry should go the way of the dinosaurs. This is especially true if there is a complete ban on advertising; the prices of your products are going through the roof; there are massive restrictions on the use of your products: how you can describe them (Light, Mild, Ultra, etc.), and what you can put in them (namely flavorings). Just one problem, as Big Tobacco has shown, losing customers can result in increased profits.

Canada is probably the best example. As you will recall, Health Canada launched a highly focused, and extremely successful, campaign to cut the number of adult smokers in half. When the effort began, 30% of adults in the country smoked. Today, the number is somewhere between 10 and 15 percent. Do the math. Half the number of customers, half the revenue.

But, as Disraeli (yes, it was Disraeli not Mark Twain) said, "There are lies, damn lies, and statistics." Half the number of customers translates to twice, if not more, revenue, not less! How? Read on because you can do it too, regardless of your industry.

The tobacco industry measures success per 1,000 sticks sold. There are 20 sticks to a pack of cigarettes, ten packs to a carton, so a thousand sticks are five cartons. For every five cartons sold, the manufacturer makes in the region of $150, although this does vary by brand and country. In any event, we are talking billions of dollars in profits because of what we call "high margins."

By comparison, in Russia, where there are few controls on the tobacco industry, a pack costs less than a dollar and manufacturers' profit on five cartons, a thousand sticks, is roughly five dollars. That is what we call "low margins."

When an industry is regulated, it is sometimes discriminatory. The regulations are on some companies, not all. There are laws in the United States, for example, pertaining to the responsibility of business owners towards their employees, but only if they have a minimum number of full-time equivalent employees. So, a company with ten employees does not have to provide them with health insurance, but a company with a thousand does, even if they are in the same industry, producing the same widgets. That is discriminatory. The playing field is not level. With Tobacco, as we have already seen, it is non-discriminatory. Everyone is treated the same.

That level playing field is the key component to profitability. In most countries no one can advertise, no one can use product descriptors, and no one can use additives.

The result is a huge savings that can all go to the bottom line. (As we will see, it can also go to other things like employee benefits.) Instead of manufacturing ten different Stock-Keeping Units (SKUs), now a company may only have two. Manufacturing costs plummet. And as packaging for the existing products is virtually identical, packaging/printing costs also plummet.

Market share remains constant. You have no new competitors and, because of the restrictions on the physical sale of your products, literally hiding them from view in stores, you have the psychological advantage of your products becoming enticing to younger people who always want what they cannot have. In other words, the government, through their restrictions, markets your product to a new generation. You don't. It's illegal for you to do it. But the government does. And you are not responsible for underage smoking. Retailers, the convenience store owners/workers who sell the products, are responsible, or those adults who buy cigarettes for children. A "We Sell Cigarettes" sign is the best advertisement of all for your product because, when a youth asks to buy, and is told it is illegal, they salivate like a Pavlovian puppy. The only thing they want more, at least the boys, than those forbidden sticks are the adult magazines hidden on the top shelves.

So, while the industry has lost half of their customers, the number of the remaining half has stayed constant. Some, sadly, die. Some, happily, quit. But regrettably, they are all replaced by younger people seeking the forbidden fruit that is nicotine and tobacco.

Of course, cigarettes are expensive. As we have seen, the culprit is the government due to the taxes they impose on the product, although the manufacturers throw in a couple of pennies for good measure. Again, in most western countries, 80% of the cost of a pack of cigarettes is one tax or another.

Now comes the important question: What would you prefer to earn, 20% of a $15 pack of cigarettes (today's cost) or 80% of one dollar (the 1964 cost)? The answer is obvious, and it is the reason for the increase in profitability.

Steve Jobs famously said, "Quality is more important than quantity. One home run is more important than two doubles."

I am not referring here to the quality of the product. Granted, as I will explain, tobacco leaves are different, but for all intents and purposes, a smoke is a smoke. For present purposes, it's the quality of the customer that is important. Allow me to explain:

While Tobacco has customers, you probably have clients. The difference between the two is that, for the most part, a business with customers does not form a personal relationship with them. You and your dry cleaner may enjoy spending a few minutes together each week, but they don't know too much about you and you certainly don't know much about them. You are their customer. On the other hand, your accountant knows everything about you and your family. You are their client.

There are great clients. They know what they want. They know how to ask for it. They don't change their mind halfway through the assignment. They are polite. They demand quality and professionalism, but they are not demanding. They are a pleasure to work with. You enjoy them. They bring a smile to your face. Oh, and they pay on time.

But then there are those clients who, if you look up the word "aggravating" in the dictionary, you will find their photo. They are demanding, not in a good way but in the worse possible way. They are always saying they need something right away. With them everything is rush, rush, rush. And they are never happy. They don't put a smile on your face, but rather a frown. Oh, and they don't pay on time.

Then, one day, one glorious day, when you are complaining to a friend about them, the friend asks, innocently as a lamb, "Why don't you fire them?" You are shocked! "They're not an employee. How can I fire a client? I can't fire a client!!"

Well, of course you can. You can also fire a customer. You've seen it. The customer who is escorted out of the store for being rude to a salesperson is being fired. The client who keeps you up at night and is giving you an ulcer can be fired. And when you fire them, you don't lose money, you earn more. How? Why?

When someone is causing you distress, unreasonable distress, not based on the complexity of the problem with which they have presented you, but on the complexity of their personality, it impacts the quality of your work for your other clients. The quality goes down. When the quality goes down, the phones go up in your clients' offices and they start looking to replace you. You lose business, and your reputation, because you did not fire that one client who was driving you crazy. So, you fire them. You sleep better. You and your staff are happier. (And none of your staff leaves, another possible ramification of having a bad client.) The quality of your work not only does not deteriorate, but it improves. All is well and fine, and your banker is extremely pleased because, as your blood pressure lowers, your bank balances rise.

But what about making money the ole fashioned way? Raising prices. Most business owners undercharge for their products and services because they are afraid to lose business. That's logical but, in fact, they are usually wrong. (I would not hesitate to say that many of the best business decisions are counter intuitive.)

The notion that if you raise prices, you will lose customers or clients, is also wrong. Yes, you will lose some. But not all of them. In fact, studies have shown that most customers will stay with the business, and any loss will be made up for by the higher prices. However, this is only if the price rise appears to be reasonable, if you can justify it if asked for an explanation. ("The government has raised taxes on cigarettes, again." "The government has increased the tariffs on imports from China and the thingamabobs I use come from China. Ironically, even with the tariffs they are still the least expensive.")

Consider this: you might be in an industry where your competitors are the big boys who are undercutting you and everyone else. In that case, you can't very well raise your prices unless you provide something that the big boys don't. For example, your widget comes with a guarantee or a service package. So, while you charge a few dollars more, the customer sees the value. And if the added value is an existing cost, there probably won't really be an added expense.

Simple example: Chain restaurants. You have a pizzeria that is located next to a chain restaurant which has name recognition and gifts for the kids.

Yours is a family restaurant. You can't compete when the kids insist on having a "Happy Meal," but you can compete on service. For example, your child has eaten half their dish of ice cream and the owner comes over and asks the child why they aren't eating the other half. So, she takes the half-full dish of ice cream away, replacing it with a full dish. No more crying for a "Happy Meal," the crying is now for the nice lady who gives more ice cream. Does the business owner lose money? Of course not! Unlike at the chain stores, satisfied customers at family restaurants leave tips.

Or another example. At this family restaurant, every time you order a dessert, a loyalty card gets stamped. Once a customer has 10 stamps, they get a free dessert. What happens? First, you may be guaranteed at least 10 visits from the customer. Second, more often than not, the customer loses the card. So, my guess is you probably wind up ahead or, at worse, break even.

When faced with the issue of whether or not to raise prices any business owner should be worried. There is the famous (or is the word "infamous?") case of Netflix which, when they raised their subscription fees disaster followed. They were able to reverse course; you may not be able to recover.

But it may not be a question of changing (raising) prices, but rather changing customers. (This brings us back to the quality of customers or clients.) The price you charge determines the type of business you want to have. Are you a discount shop? Nothing wrong with that. Are you a premium shop? Nothing wrong with that. But the people, and they are all good people, who come into your store will be different. No one goes into a discount shop wearing an Armani suit, and no one goes into Tiffany wearing a potato sack.

Of course, moving from discount to premium also means creating new expectations. Can you meet them? No one paying a dollar for a pack of four stick pens expects any type of warranty. On the other hand, if someone is paying a few hundred dollars for a fountain pen named after a mountain in Switzerland, well, let's just say that it better not leak.

Besides needing more money to survive, or wanting more money to provide yourself and your family with luxuries, there is a practical reason to raise prices. You want to grow your business. Simple. Straight forward. No further explanation needed.

But you have a problem. You are limited to the number of things you can offer your customers or clients. If you are a brick-and-mortar store, without an ecommerce website, you have a limited amount of shelf- and storage-space. If you are a service provider, you do what you do and can't do any more. You're a plumber. That's it. So, raising prices is the only way to grow your business. Not having a choice can make a decision a great deal easier.

Raising prices does not necessarily mean adding on a certain percentage to everything you offer. You could actually lower your prices on some service packages and raise the price on others. (This goes back to the differentiation between discount and premium.)

Think of cereal. You go to the supermarket and reach for your favorite name brand breakfast food. Located right beside it, for much less, is the supermarket's brand. You get curious. You read the ingredients on both boxes, and you discover that they are identical. In fact, if you did some research, you might very well discover that they are manufactured in the same factory! The brand name manufacturer sells to their competitor, the supermarket selling a generic brand. The difference between the two? The size of the box. The printing on the box. And the price of the box. What is not different is the contents of the box.

Cereal, of course, is not a luxury item. So, what about diamonds? You can't get more luxury than that. The diamond industry is dirty in more ways than one. There is a lot of human suffering in every sparkle of that diamond in the ring you dished out thousands to buy for the love of your life.

There is a brand-new industry, artificial diamonds as shiny and as hard as the real things but costing only one-one thousandth of the price. I am not talking about cubic zirconia but rather artificial, meaning man-made, diamonds. Sensing a threat to their business, what did DeBeers do? They started manufacturing the fakes themselves and, most importantly, undercutting their rivals. The result, seeing how inexpensive they are, customers think they are also cheap. No one wants to buy a cheap diamond. In other words, just like the name-brand cereal manufacturers, DeBeers is making generic diamonds to protect their market share and to put their competitors out of business (which, of course, the name brand cereal manufacturers don't do to the supermarket brands because they want the choice between the products to be bold and visible. And, who knows, maybe one day, as a treat for the kids, instead of buying the generic, the parents will buy the name brand.).

So why in the world would anyone, with an iota of common sense, pay more for the same thing they can get for much cheaper? Let's call it "the snob factor." *Those people* buy that product. *Those people* eat at those restaurants. *Those people*...well, you get the idea, and you know the people who make those statements and who the "*those people*" are to whom they are referring. Snobs. But it works.

In the UK, there is a food chain, sort of a bakery cum eatery, named Greggs. It sells simple fare. The food is inexpensive, not of the highest quality, but there is always a line to get into their stores. People make jokes about Greggs and their clientele. You know, *those people*. The "working class."

So, the marketing agency at Greggs came up with an idea. The chain sells steak and chicken in puff pastry, amongst many other baked delights. They set up a stall at a farmers' market in a well-to-do neighborhood in England. They changed the packaging, napkins, labeling, everything, including the name. It was no longer "Greggs" but was now "Patisserie Gregoire." Same food. Same contents. Same everything except for the name and the incidentals. So, what happened? The very people who would not have been caught dead in a Greggs store were exclaiming that the food, "tastes like it comes from the streets of Paris." Snobs.

Impression, sometimes, is reality. By having the generic brand next to their name brand product, the manufacturer of the latter allows a contrast with the former. Charging more means that the person buying it isn't foolish, but successful. They can afford the more expensive brand; those people cannot.

By raising your prices, you may be inviting people to feel that they are in an exclusive club.

What's the difference between a Chevy and a BMW? Both will get you from point A to point B. Both are relatively safe. (You can die in a $50,000 BMW just like in a $20,000 Chevy.) But one is a status symbol while the other isn't. Snobs.

The point is, that when you raise your prices, you may lose some customers or clients, but you will become a "luxury brand" and be able to sell less to richer clients than more to poorer clients. Think of it this way: To sell to a mass audience the manufacturer has to "dumb down" the product by lowering the price and the money they spend on packaging and marketing. On the other hand, when you are only targeting a small segment of the population, the rich, you spend the money on packaging and marketing because that is what luxury is all about. Quality costs more. Higher prices equate to higher quality and value.

With cigarettes the quality is the quality of the tobacco, paper vs. paper, filter vs. filter. All of which are subjective. You like what you like. What is not subjective is the fact that the quality of a product or service replaces the brand. Perhaps the best example is Volvo.

Everyone knows that Volvo stands for safety. I am of course exaggerating but, when you drive a Volvo, you are practically driving a tank. Your family will be safe in one of those cars. No one knows the tag line for Volvo. Without checking, I don't even know if they have one. But I know that their reputation is safety and therefore, all things being equal, if I am only interested in safety, I'm buying a Volvo.

And this brings me to the crucial difference between client acquisition and client retention.

Quoting from the website markinblog.com:

- *The probability of selling to an existing customer is 60-70%, while the probability of selling to a new prospect is only 5% to 20%.*
- *It costs up to 7x more to acquire a new customer than to retain an old one.*
- *Increasing customer retention by 5% increases profits by 25-29%.*
- *44% of companies have a greater focus on acquisition vs. 16% that focus on retention.*

- *65% of a company's business comes from existing customers.*
- *For most industries, the average customer retention rate is below 20%.*
- *Loyal customers spend 67% more than new ones.*
- *Only 40% of companies and 30% of agencies have an equal focus on acquisition and retention.*
- *89% of [businesses] see customer experience as a key factor in driving customer loyalty and retention.*
- *Existing customers are 50% more likely to try new products and spend 31% more than new customers.*
- *82% of companies agree that customer retention is cheaper than acquisition.*

The one resource you have that is finite, limited and you cannot increase is - time. Having read the above 11 points, how would you rather spend your time, running after new clients or doing all you can to hold on to the ones you already have?

It's not even really a question. No one doubts or argues about the answer. Of course, you still need a pipeline and to have a few new clients to replace the ones you will inevitably lose, but your emphasis must be on client retention, not acquisition.

Now, because you raised your prices or fired your bad clients, you have fewer clients, or customers, and you can devote more of your time to each. It is a better, more cost-effective, and a more profitable use of that most limited of your resources.

A good analogy may be the airline industry. When they cut an unprofitable route, they can devote more to the remaining routes, enabling them to better compete with their competitors. And they raise their prices.

All business owners have heard of the 80/20 rule. Eighty percent of revenue comes from 20% of customers. Well, the same can be said for aggravation, stress, and lost time. Twenty per cent of your customers/clients cause 80% of your aggravation and stress and take up 80% of your time.

Since you are now being more attentive to your fewer clients, those clients can become your free sales or marketing team. They sing your praises. When someone compliments them on the work you did for them, they refer them to you. There is no better referral than a recommendation from a happy client. Always remember, the most effective and cheapest salesforce are your current customers/clients.

In a way, it's the same with cigarettes. Since there is no substantial difference between smokes, if someone prefers the smell of another person's cigarette, cigar, or pipe tobacco, to their own, they will ask them what they are smoking. That's another way tobacco companies get new customers, not new smokers, new customers.

And, to further shock you, you will shortly learn about a new brand of cigarette that are "safer," FDA approved, and may be attempting to prove a new adage, it is not "fewer customers, more profit," but "less nicotine, more profit!"

SOURCES:

Raising Prices:
https://www.growthramp.io/articles/price-increase
https://www.forbes.com/sites/theyec/2011/12/28/5-business-lessons-from-the-netflix-pricing-debacle/?sh=723fce4dd2a7
https://www.liveagent.com/blog/tips-to-boost-customer-happiness/
https://www.quicksprout.com/psychological-pricing/

Customer Acquisition:
https://www.markinblog.com/customer-loyalty-retention-statistics/

CHAPTER 4:
WHAT THEY DON'T TEACH YOU IN BUSINESS SCHOOL

There are numerous and varied tricks, or gimmicks, that most companies use to get people to buy their products, not just the Tobacco industry. They are all perfectly legal and proven to be effective. I am willing to wager that you, yourself, have probably been the target of some of these strategies. And there is nothing wrong with that. We all have.

Why? Because companies use psychology to reel us in like fish on a hook. They want to make us think we need something even though we probably don't. They create the need in our mind and reap the financial rewards.

Let's consider, in no specific order, a dozen of these methods, which I again reiterate, are totally legal:

You're Family

"I only smoke Marlboros." Period. End of sentence. You ask the man what he smokes, "Marlboro." You ask the woman what she smokes, "Camel." That is what the tobacco companies wanted. That is what they got. Loyalty. Even though the difference between brands of cigarettes is negligible, think Coke and Pepsi, people are loyal to their brand. The branding is the major difference in the product not the actual ingredients. It is all about the bond that is created with the customer.

That did not just mean they would always purchase that brand, far more importantly, they would always recommend their brand (note the significance of the emphasis), to friends and relatives. There is no better salesperson than a friend or relative because, statistically, a person will almost always purchase something recommended by someone they trust, a friend or relative, rather than something recommended by a stranger.

But it's not just cigarettes. Even today, in some parts of Brooklyn, you never mention the Dodgers! That is also brand loyalty.

An Apple computer user would not be caught dead with a PC. That's brand loyalty. When General Motors decided to discontinue their Saturn cars, owners mourned, almost literally. Some were so outraged at the betrayal that they swore they would never buy a GM car again. That's brand loyalty. In fact, simply to reinforce the bond with their customers, Saturn dealerships would have events for them and their families which the car owners would gladly attend alone or with their spouse and children. Who spends a beautiful Saturday or Sunday at a picnic at a car dealership? A loyal customer.

They achieve brand loyalty by not only offering a quality product that the individual truly likes, but by making the brand into a club. Companies, in general, may sell baseball caps, shirts, bags, pens, tote bags, gym bags, whatever, with the brand's logo on them. Free marketing with people paying a premium price for things they don't need and would otherwise, were it not for their pride in being a user of the brand, buy, wear or use.

Everybody's Doing It

As with friends and family recommendations, companies advertise their products in such a way that it makes a person who does not buy their products feel like an outsider. If "nine out of 10" dentists recommend it, it must be good. If 90% of high school students recommend this anti-acne cream, it must be good. If 95% of customers renew their subscription for the latest over-the-counter-drug-free medicine, created by a real doctor, it must be good. If everybody else is buying it, it must be good. (Remember the "Everybody's doing it, Skidoo" commercials?) And if it must be good, of course you are going to buy it.

This is really nothing more than glorified peer pressure. With Tobacco it was something like, "Nine out of 10 smokers prefer the taste of this low tar cigarette to the regular cigarette." It worked for Tobacco just like everyone else.

The Best Medicine

Tobacco had Joe Camel and his family. They were cartoons on commercials designed to make people laugh. Go to YouTube and find the Hamlet Cigar commercials which were for, you guessed it, British cigars. You may find yourself falling off your chair laughing. The theme of the commercials was "solace in the face of adversity."

Mention Budweiser to some people and they may say "the King of Beers." Others might talk about the sentimental Super Bowl commercial when Clydesdale meets puppy. Or they might remember the other tearjerker with returning veterans. Or they might talk about the frogs, and smile.

Forget about beer. Let's take a serious subject: insurance. Mention Geico and people think of the gecko. Mention Progressive and people think of Fran. Or it could be the emu in Liberty Mutual commercials. And we cannot forget the Aflac duck. People remember funny ads.

The best medicine, as they say, is humor. If you are in a good mood, you are more likely to buy. Humor, or sentimentality, is thus a great marketing tool. If an advertiser can get you to laugh, or cry, you will remember the product they are hawking and buy it. Get a tear; get a chuckle; make a sale. That's why Super Bowl commercials are so funny and so expensive.

The Flight or Fight Response

It's human nature: See a puppy and bend over and pet the little fellow. See a snake and either freeze in fear or run for the hills. It is a visceral and natural response that has kept humanity alive for millennia. And it is a great sales tactic. (By the way, if you are counting, this counts as two of the 12 methods I promised you.)

"Limited time only." "While supplies last." "Today only." In other words, you better buy it now or you may never be able to get it again. Tobacco did it by limiting the availability of flavored cigarettes, or releasing retro packing, etc. Fast food chains do it. They introduce a new or limited time product (such as the McRib) and then withdraw it. When it comes back, you rush to get it before it is gone. You are afraid of missing out. Social media even has an acronym for it: FOMO. And just as it works on-line, it works in stores. It is creating the illusion of scarcity.

Of course, you don't really have to be afraid of not getting that 2,000-calorie indulgence. In fact, you probably should be afraid of getting it! But there are real monsters out there of whom you should be afraid.

Well, not to worry. After telling you about the crime statistics, or betting that you have been watching the news, the security company whose ad you are watching, offers safety for yourself, your family, and your property. And it's simple, you can even install it yourself. And all you have to pay is a low monthly monitoring fee and you can literally rest easy. The ad you are watching comes with a code you can use to get a month's monitoring for free. But you better act now before the code is gone! Sound familiar?

As for Tobacco, it wasn't actually fear, but more anger, although they are different sides of the same coin. With Tobacco it, obviously, was not fear of the product but fear, anger if you will, of the government telling you, an adult, what you can and cannot do. If today they are telling you that you can't smoke, what will it be tomorrow?

Mark Downs

You have seen the signs, "Was $999.99. Now Only $499.99." You would be a fool not to buy at that price. Anyone can do the math in their heads. Five hundred off! Wow! Compare the numbers! What is there to think about?

Well, two things: First, you came into the store to buy a belt, not a television. So, you are being enticed by comparison shopping, not of different products mind you, but one product with two different prices, the old higher one and the new lower one. Second, technically they are not lying. The price was $999.99. It's just that that was the sign on the one television, same model mind you, that they stuck on the back shelf two weeks ago and no one saw, and no one bought because they saw other models for less if they even saw that particular model at all.

The store never intended to sell it for a thousand bucks. They wanted to sell it for five hundred and now you, and a lot of other people, have fallen into the trap. Truth is, it's not a good deal but you don't care because you think it is. You leave with a smile on your face almost as big as that on the face of the owner of the store.

For the record, tobacco companies' version of this was called OPF, Overprinted Film, on which was written "Previously $5 a Pack, Now Only $4" or "Buy a carton, get a pack for free." Which brings me to…

It's FREE!

"There is no such thing as a free lunch." But we all like to think they are free, so we sign up. (This is why "freemiums" became so popular with online services.) After all, the company makes it clear that you can cancel at any time before the subscription ends. This could be for an anti-virus program for your computers or a membership in some shopping club like Amazon Prime. After all, if Mr. Bezos is generous enough to let you get your packages delivered the same day or within a day, for free, for 30-days, what's the harm?

There is none. Of course, you really don't need anything within 24 to 48 hours. If there was something, you would get in the car, or hop on a ride service, or take the bus, and buy it. But why go to "it" when "it" can be brought to you? For free. For 30 days. Then you will cancel.

Well, you might very well cancel but, when you do, they will offer you an extension at a low price or for free. So, the clock, so to speak, starts anew.

Of course, you might forget to cancel and not pay any attention to your credit card bill and, next thing you know, you have been using the no-longer-free service for a few months and are now hooked. Or, you may actually like the service, want the service, but don't need the service, and yet still buy the subscription which, after a while, you won't need any more because you have nothing to buy, but you still like the perks that come with the subscription, such as access to a streaming service which you got hooked on, because it was "free" and now you can't live without it.

So, you now are paying for free one-day delivery that you don't need and a streaming service that you never wanted.

In any event, the tobacco industry championed the idea of giving product away for free to capture customers. There is nothing new here.

Number Confusion

Sometimes math *is* required.

You want to buy a big-ticket item. It could be a car, a boat, a home entertainment system, a computer with all the bells and whistles. This time we are not talking about something you don't need and are being enticed to buy, but rather something you need. The question is, Which do you buy?

For sake of argument, you have three options. Because the store wants your business, they focus on two things: price and "something else." In the case of a car or boat, the "something else" may be a warranty. In the case of the entertainment system and the computer, it's a warranty of a different type, a service package. But, for our purposes, it's all the same thing, a warranty. Let's use the computer as the example.

You go into your local computer chain store and they offer you a $3,000 computer, with all the bells and whistles, most of which you do not need and may not understand, but it comes with a life time subscription to Office 365 and to their service package according to which, remotely or in-store, they promise to fix whatever happens to the computer as long as you don't pour liquid on it or drop it.

But the salesperson, being a well-trained salesperson, says, "Well, maybe you don't need all the bells and whistles. We have a very good computer for $1,500 that will meet all your needs and comes with Office 365 and our service package for one-year." Sounds good to you. But wait, there's more!

Before you say, "I'll take it," the salesperson shows you a third option: For just $500 more, you get a computer that, like the $3,000 computer, runs at the speed of light (the $1,500 model only goes at the speed of sound), and gives you Office 365 and the service package for two years. This, the $2,000 computer, is a decoy. Compared to the $1,500 offer, it's a good deal. But compared to the $3,000 computer, it's not. So, you buy the $3,000 computer even though you really don't need it.

The decoy used by Tobacco is to have multiple products/brands to make their premium brand, the one they want you to buy, look like a better deal because the "value" brands that they offer are clearly, at least if you go by the packaging, in those jurisdictions that still allow real packaging, look cheap while the others look like quality. Or the decoy may be the name. The customer has never heard of "Classic" or "Basic" and does not want to smoke it. But the brand name, Marlboro, that they will smoke because they have heard of it.

Don't Worry, Be Happy

This is all about appealing to your emotions. It's emotional not factual. In the case of Hamlet Cigars, the tag line was "Happiness is a Hamlet Cigar." And, in conjunction with their advertising campaign commercials, which I hope you will take time to watch, it worked. The same was true for the general message sent through their marketing that smoking will give you pleasure. Ultimately, all commercials are about making the consumer happy. No one is going to buy something that will make them sad! Donate to a worthwhile charity, yes. Buy something, no.

Take the following scenario for example: You have a serious problem which is causing you stress. You are not alone. It is a common condition. It is so common a condition that they advertise a solution, a cure, on television. You are vulnerable. Everything on the commercial sounds and looks like a dream come true. The answer to your prayers. And you pick up the phone, call the 800 number, or log on to the website, and buy. There is nothing new here. Tonics, perhaps the most famous being Coca-Cola, as I already reminded you, originally contained cocaine, promised to cure everything from cancer to arthritis. People fell for it back in the day, and they fall for it now. Why? Because they are desperate and desperate people do desperate things. They are looking for quality of life and the product seems to be the answer. But there's another reason, which brings me to the next method.

Look Who It Is!

One of the most effective sales/marketing tricks is the celebrity endorsement. Get a celeb to wear your product, to use your product, to be seen with your product, have their picture with it posted online, and you better be ready for your website to crash. Everybody and their brother or sister, as the case may be, will want to buy your widget.

Or better yet, get a celeb to hawk your product on television and then be prepared to handle a great volume of business. Actors and athletes are probably the best celebrities to hire. No one asks if they really use the product. No one asks what they know about the product. All they know is the actor can read lines with emotion and the athlete can score points with consistency and that's good enough for them. For some strange reason, actors and athletes are trusted. So, consumers buy from someone who may not use the product, may not understand the product, and is being paid to convince them to buy it. (If they are being paid, mention may have to be made on the ad, usually in writing, usually very small writing!) Silly, isn't it?

Tobacco, at first used celebrities but, when they could no longer do so, they used authorities such as physicians. Strange but true.

Fantasy

Perhaps the best sales/marketing method is creating a fantasy. But not any fantasy, a sexual fantasy. Procreation, like fear, is part of our primitive brain. We are literally drawn to the "beautiful people." Sex has always, and will always, sell. Except, as with Hamlet, the main character in a Tobacco ad or, for that matter, a cartoon character, all the Tobacco ads featured attractive people, such as the Marlboro Man and the Virginia Slims women.

Here's the mentality: Look at that model! She's gorgeous! If I buy the jeans she is wearing, I'll look just like her and have everything she has! Yah, right. Look at him! Look at how all those women are staring at him. If I buy that car, watch, suit, women will be all over me just like they're all over him! Yah, right.

But it works.

Once Upon a Time

Lastly, there is nothing better than a good story, a narrative that creates emotions. Don't misunderstand, the best stories are true. But true or false, storytelling sells. All tobacco brands had a story around them, most famously, the mystic of the Marlboro Man or the independence of the Virginia Slims-smoking woman. It is the story around the brand that does the selling.

When a salesperson tells a potential buyer a story that resonates with them, it shows that the salesperson has been listening when they explained what they wanted and why, and a connection is immediately formed. Of course, the story will always have a happy ending. The person in the story, just like them, the customer, bought the whatever and raves about it because it worked. It solved their problem which also happens to be your problem. Not a celebrity mind you, but a regular person just like them.

Stories relax you. They put you at ease. That's why bedtime stories put children to sleep and reading in bed puts adults to sleep. And when you are relaxed, after hearing a story of a successful sale, you are more likely to buy.

Again, all these marketing methods are simple psychology. You are being conned, but you know it, and you don't mind. Because it is just too good for you to walk away

CHAPTER 5: TAX ME MORE, PLEASE

It does not make any sense, at least at first blush, but it is quite true that the more you are taxed the more profit you can earn. This can be done in three ways: Piggybacking on taxation, collecting taxes for the government, or transfer pricing.

Piggybacking

In economic terms, tobacco is one of the most inelastic products on the market. People will buy it, regardless of the price, because they are addicted to it (meaning the nicotine). Their brain literally tells them, "You need this."

When Tobacco became a target of the government, the government had a problem. The vast majority of smokers were adults. And those youth who were smokers would, if they survived, become adults. Another word for "adult" is "voter." Regardless of party affiliation or political philosophy, all persons in government agree on one thing: It is not wise to aggravate voters. Do that, and they will no longer be your voters. On the other hand, the government had to act to fight smoking. But how?

Let's call it, "The Lobster Approach." You place a live lobster in a pot of water, turn the heat on and, because it is gradual, the lobster does not sense the danger. Before it knows it, it's being served with butter sauce. In other words, a modified KISS approach. But instead of Keep it Simple Stupid, now it's Keep it Slow Stupid.

And that's what the government did. They began with a small tax and an explanation that they needed the money to help the health system recoup losses caused by the number of smoking-related illnesses. Drivers, paying a gas tax, are paying for repairs to the transportation infrastructure. In the case of tobacco, it's the same thing. Smokers are paying, if you will, for repairs to the health care system. And the tax is so small, who cares? And it's logical: If you smoke, you pay; if you don't smoke, you don't pay. If you drive, you pay; if you don't drive, you don't pay. Same thing.

Over time, just like our friend the lobster, before they knew it, the smoker was in a boiling pot of taxes. They were paying $15 to $20 for a pack of cigarettes, 80% of which was a tax of one kind or another. (Pardon the repetition.) How crazy is this? Again, $20 for what? For a box of dried leaves and paper! After all, that's what a cigarette is. So, the retail price of a pack bears very little resemblance to the actual cost of the product. And, again, just like any addict, regardless of price, the smoker will find a way to pay for their "fix," even if they have to turn to the black market.

There are $5 packs of cigarettes. Some are gray market imports. These are real cigarettes illegally brought into the country. For sake of argument, let's say that country A has no tax on cigarettes. They import the good stuff. A citizen from country B visits that country, purchases 1,000 cartons, ships them home and sells them at an astronomical markup but still less than his fellow citizens pay for their cigarettes. Those are "gray" cigarettes.

Then there are the counterfeits. Smokers immediately know they are not the real thing because they smell horrible, taste even worse, and irritate their throats causing them to cough more than usual. But, instead of paying $15 a pack, they pay $5. Still, they need their fix, and they are getting it. Throw in a little cognitive dissonance, and they convince themselves that the garbage (to use a polite term) they are smoking isn't really that bad.

The point is, that while there are many people who want to quit smoking, and should be encouraged to do so (a million succeed each year), there are possibly many more who simply do not because, despite understanding the possible (likely?) ramifications, they do not want to quit what they consider to be a delightful habit. For them, it is pleasurable.

The truth is, as the taxes on cigarettes increased the number of smokers decreased, because they quit or, sadly, died. The hard truth is, that as the number of smokers decreased, so did their influence on politicians. Fewer smokers meant fewer voters. And fewer votes meant less influence on the political system. Here come the taxes.

But that's not all, even smokers without nagging friends and relatives pressuring them to quit, still had to deal with the institutionalized shaming resulting from the change in societal norms brought on, in no small part, by government anti-smoking campaigns. As a result, smokers would say that they were going to quit, "when the price of a pack increases again." Except for a small fraction, they never did.

The government found a way to make the public comfortable with increased taxes without aggravating the electorate. The smoker did not complain because of the shaming. And the non-smoker did not complain because they believed smokers should pay more for the harm they were causing the health care system. (The fact, as I have shown, that they were actually saving the social network, was irrelevant because that was never pointed out by anyone.) The non-smokers, let alone the smokers, never thought that this could be a precedent for something else. They never even thought about the similarities with gasoline. So first it was gas, then it was tobacco. What's next? They never asked. No one did.

As you will recall, as the government raised taxes, manufacturers added a few pennies to the cost. So, once, twice, or even three times a year, manufacturers were able to earn more for their products without the consumer complaining because the government took all the blame. Even though they had half the customers as before, tobacco companies were now earning 20% of a, for sake of argument, $15 pack of cigarettes (the other 80% going to the government) which was substantially more favorable for them than when they were earning 90% of a one-dollar pack of cigarettes. And that is why tobacco companies are so financially successful even though they have lost half their customers.

But that is not exactly accurate. While in North American and Europe half of their customers are gone, worldwide more people are smoking. However, because the taxes are so low outside of North America and Europe, and even though it is in those countries where demand for product has increased that the taxes are low or non-existent, it is in the heavily taxed countries where tobacco manufacturers are earning the bulk of their profits.

Canada, which arguably has the most draconian laws regulating tobacco of any country in the world, is one of the most profitable countries for the industry. Why? Market share is protected and constant increases in tax means the constant increase in the few cents manufacturers can add to the price.

The irony is not only that higher taxes mean higher profits. It is also ironic that the increased profits in the, let's call them, the anti-smoking countries, means that manufacturers have the financial resources to legally advertise, market and promote their products in the lower- or non-taxed countries where demand for product is increasing.

We cannot forget that the government is earning a fortune from taxes. This means that the Tobacco industry is their Golden Goose, and no one kills a Golden Goose. They protect it, in this case by solidifying market share through the restriction of advertising, which also means that companies' former marketing budgets can go directly to their bottom lines. What future Golden Geese may the government be grooming?

Sugary drinks. Bad for you. Are taxes coming? Alcohol. Bad for you. Are more taxes coming? What about an "environmental" tax on fuel or a "recycling" tax? We have to protect the environment, don't we? If this should happen, each of these industries will follow the example of Tobacco. When the government raises or imposes taxes on their products, they will sneak in a couple of cents for good measure and better profits. If Tobacco made lemonade out of lemons, why not an actual sugary drink manufacturer?

Before continuing, let's consider the "environmental" tax. As previously mentioned, electric vehicles are all the rage. They do not pollute. Or do they? Relatively few households get all of their electricity from renewable sources of energy (hydro, wind, solar). So where does the remaining electricity come from? Fossil fuels. So, when an owner of an EV is filling up their "tank," some of it is fuel, albeit in the form of electrons and not liquid.

More importantly are those batteries that make the EV run. They all need two things: cobalt and nickel. The good news is, there is more cobalt and nickel in North American than all Americans and Canadians could ever use. The bad news is, to mine it would cause an environmental disaster, using current methods. So, to where do we go to get our cobalt and nickel? The two countries not exactly known for being environmentally conscientious: Russia, which mines the cobalt, and China, which processes the Russian cobalt and also extracts the nickel from sub-Saharan African countries who have sold it the mining rights. In other words, there is a lot of pollution in a "tank" of EV "fuel."

Of course, very few people realize this. So, what may happen? The government will explain the problem to their citizens. They will then say that in order to safely mine and process the vital minerals at home, new mining techniques have to be developed. And then, once again, slowly, they will start taxing, increasing the amount in increments, until an EV battery costs hundreds of dollars more than the Sino-Russian counterpart. And being loyal Americans, Canadians, Brits, etc., no one will complain because paying a higher price is patriotic, good for the country and good for the planet. The fact that the Russians and Chinese will continue to pollute like there is no tomorrow, will be an inconvenience best ignored. And the battery manufacturers will do exactly what Tobacco did, except instead of adding a few pennies to the cost of their batteries every time the government raises the "environmental" tax, they'll add a few bucks, or loonies, or quid, as the case may be. The companies will make money, and the government will make a lot of money and have a new Golden Goose to protect (only this new Goose will be compensating it for the loss of the previous Goose, the gasoline tax).

Don't think for a minute that this can't happen. It is happening today, and has been happening for a long time, with the airline industry. A tax is technically what is called an "impot," which is a tax on a person, such as an income tax, a poll tax, or a property tax. What, in the case of the airlines, for example, makes this tax unique is that it is hidden in plain view.

Look at an old receipt for an airline ticket, or look at a new one. On one side will appear the cost of the flight. Simple enough. But on the other you will find "the passenger service charge" which will include real taxes, money that goes to the government, but also things like a fuel surcharge, a convenience fee, or possibly a security charge. None of these goes to the government. They are not taxes. The airline keeps that money. And who is blamed for these extra charges over and above what was charged for the actual flight? The government. Since consumers figure it is the government that is ripping them off and not the airlines, they don't complain.

This is analogous to "shipping and handling" fees. Have you ever purchased a widget "for free + S & H?" Of course, you have. Now the shipping costs are legit. The price of an envelope, label and stamp are the price of an envelope, label and stamp. Let's say together they cost $2 (which is probably an exaggeration). The "handling fee," meaning the price you are paying for the "free" widget to be placed in the envelope, have the shipping label affixed to it, along with the stamp, and mailed, is $12. Does it really cost $12? Of course not. But that's how the company is able to give it away "for free." It's not free, you are paying a good $10 for it, and "it" probably comes from China and only costs a couple of bucks, if that, to manufacture and ship to the US. In this way, companies create their own "tax," in a manner of speaking.

Again, when it is a real tax, the government is getting the money. If it is a lot of money, meaning of significant value to the government, the government will protect the product. As I already said, in the case of the UK, if the government were to get rid of all taxes on tobacco products, income tax would have to be increased by around 11%. In Canada and the US, it would probably be a 10% increase. You don't need a Ph.D. in Political Science to know what would happen to any government that would make such a move.

So, if in the eyes of the government your product is valuable, meaning they will be earning a lot of revenue from the sale of that product, don't fight them if they want to raise the tax on its sale. Celebrate the increase! It means that the government is going to protect you and you can add your own impots for which the government will be blamed. It is a cash cow for everyone except, of course, the consumer.

Collecting Tax Revenue

Want to be a bank? Collect taxes for the government.

In Britain there are wholesalers known as "Cash & Carry"s. What does a Cash & Carry do? In the case of Tobacco, it takes possession of thousands of cartons of cigarettes and sells them to retailers. The British government mandates that a Value Added Tax (VAT) be imposed on each pack sold. It is the responsibility of the manufacturer to add the taxes and duties to the price, but not the VAT. So, the wholesaler, the Cash & Carry, when they sell the product to the retailer, collects the VAT for the first time (which at the time of writing this is 20% of the purchase price). This is where things get interesting.

The Cash & Carry has all this money, in cash mind you, that is meant for the government. But they do not have to turn the money over to the government for a period of time. It may be 30 days, 60 days, 90 days or even a year.

So, what to do with all that money, which could be millions? Well, for all intents and purposes, it is a free short-term loan. It can be used to increase inventory, hire more people, renovate facilities, or, for example in the case of General Electric, create a new company, GE Finance, and loan the money out. GE Finance is actually more lucrative than any other GE company. GE is a bank. Any collector of taxes can be a bank. They will have a continuous revolving revenue stream and, as long as they pay the government on time, the government will not care.

This is in fact why Cash & Carrys, or any wholesaler, can purchase cigarettes. Without the taxes, it would not pay to deal with them due to their low margins. But with the taxes, the profits are enormous.

Once again, don't be afraid of high taxes on your products. If you are able to hold on to the tax money, and the product is continuously being purchased, you could be earning some serious profits.

Transfer Pricing

So, you can make good money by piggybacking on government taxes or by collecting and holding on to tax revenues until they have to be paid to the government. Or you could do something else. You could become an international corporation, just like numerous companies that you think are national but are not.

Philip Morris International is not an American company, it's Swiss. IKEA is not Swedish, it's also Swiss.

The technical term is "transfer pricing." It is complex to do but, hopefully, not to explain.

What you do, and tobacco companies are masters at this, is to take your profitability to lower tax jurisdictions. The corporate tax rate in the US is too high? No problem. Move to Switzerland. There is just one condition: Regardless of where you manufacture your products, you have to sell them in more than one country.

Not to get ahead of myself, if you should decide to repatriate the money, your profits, and move them back to the US, yes, you will have to pay taxes on that money. But the funny thing is, because you have been paying lower or no corporate tax abroad, you will have more than enough to pay the tax on the repatriated funds.

Use your favorite multinational coffee shop as an example.

It is in every country (pretty much) and on every street corner (in some cities, almost literally). One day, we'll call it Acme Coffee USA, decided to form a Swiss holding company and sold its assets to Acme Coffee Switzerland. Acme Switzerland formed operating companies in every country where they wanted to operate. So, Acme Switzerland formed Acme USA, Acme Canada, Acme UK, etc., etc., etc.

The original Acme, Acme USA, "sold" all of its intellectual property to Acme Switzerland. But the Swiss are very nice people, so they licensed all of that intellectual property back to Acme USA. Acme USA purchases everything it can from Acme Switzerland, which probably sells everything to them at a premium. For sake of argument let's say Acme USA has revenue of $100 million a year. From that it has to pay for rent, employee salaries, and products it buys locally such as milk, pastry, cold drinks, and paper- or plasticware. And let's say, that all the USA expenses come to $70 million. That means their profits are $30 million on which they will have to pay corporate tax in the US. But that is not how this perfectly legal game is played.

For the licenses to use its intellectual property, the Swiss charge $30 million. That's $30 million for the use of logos, recipes, websites, trademarks, etc., etc., etc. Now the IRS is not going to be happy with Acme USA showing no profits. So, to keep them happy, the Swiss only charge $25 million, meaning that Acme USA has a $5 million profit.

Taxes are only a problem if you have to pay them. If you can transfer your profits to a foreign jurisdiction, where there are little to no corporate taxes, the problem is solved. (The foreign country is happy just collecting all the non-corporate taxes that businesses have to pay.)

Again, this is all perfectly legal (although, to be completely transparent, there are many more nuanccs to this process to make it legal and acceptable). Moreover, this does not mean that Acme USA is not paying any taxes in the US. They are. They have to pay employment taxes and, because they have employees, the government collects income tax. In addition to payroll taxes, the states in which they operate may collect sales tax on all, or most, of their products. The company is supporting the country's social safety network like any good corporate citizen. It is only the profitability element that is being transferred to another jurisdiction. This is what I call, "making money by saving money."

Let's get back to Philip Morris. The company was historically located in Richmond, Virginia. For the tax benefits I just described, they decided to move their international (non-US) business to Lausanne, Switzerland. But it was not just to avoid high corporate taxes. They were worried, pre-MSA, about punitive damages being awarded to litigants in civil suits filed against them. So, they moved to Switzerland to be protected from civil suit awards that could destroy the company.

Of course, it's not that simple. First, they had to negotiate with the Swiss. I have already said the Swiss are nice, but they are not foolish. They are savvy businesspeople. Philip Morris made a deal with them that they would move to Switzerland in exchange for having to pay no corporate tax in the early years. They explained that eventually they would pay but, in the meantime, they would be employing thousands of Swiss nationals. The Swiss agreed. The IRS, not so much.

The IRS was not going to allow Philip Morris to transfer ownership of its assets to a Swiss holding company, without applying some sort of tax consequences. Those assets were worth billions of dollars, perhaps trillions. Transferring them for free to their Swiss international company was not going to fly. So, the IRS said it was a sale, subject to capital gains taxes, and Philip Morris had to pay millions to make the deal go through. Without having to pay corporate taxes in Switzerland, Philip Morris had the money to pay the IRS. The Swiss were happy because they now had thousands of their citizens employed and paying taxes. The IRS was happy because they got their money. And Philip Morris was happy because, at the end of the day, even after paying the IRS they had more money than if they had stayed in the US and paid corporate taxes.

The problem that Philip Morris faced was, obviously, the IRS. And the IRS was a problem because Philip Morris is very big and very valuable. From the perspective of the IRS, Philip Morris was a great customer, and they were not going to lose them quietly. Accordingly, if you are a small business, planning on growing, selling your products in multiple countries, and realistically believe that setting up a holding company in a low corporate tax country will be to your advantage, the lesson of Philip Morris is to do so early, before you are a significant customer of the IRS. Waiting could cost you millions.

The bottom line is, do not fear taxation. It can protect you, it can help to significantly raise your revenue, and will prove the adage, "A penny saved is a penny earned."

CHAPTER 6: DON'T FEAR REGULATION

Regulation is not a dirty word. Handled correctly, it can be a blessing in disguise. The modern tobacco industry has been regulated since the mid-1960s. The severity of current regulations vary considerably by country. It all began with restrictions on advertising.

Advertising

How to go about regulating the tobacco industry? That was the question the government set out to answer. The belief was that the best way was to restrict their ability to communicate with their customers and prospective customers.

At first, the industry tried to stop them. They were confrontational. Their natural inclination was that they had to advertise, after all, if no one knew about their products, no matter how great they might be, they could not stay in business. From their perspective, that was totally logical and rational and true for every business. So, the industry decided to stand up for their rights. After all, you can't run a business and sell your products if no one knows about you or them. You have to be able to communicate with your customers.

After a while, cooler heads realized a flaw in the logic: In an environment where all companies in the industry are not allowed to advertise their products, to communicate with their customers and potential customers, then:

First, everyone in the industry is on an even playing field. No one has an advantage over anyone else.

Second, market share is protected as it is unlikely that customers will change to new/different brands, because new brands cannot advertise either. Moreover, no new manufacturers will be able to enter the industry because no one will know that they exist.

Third, the money that would have gone to advertising can go to other things, such as Research and Development. In the case of Tobacco, this meant creating replacement products for nicotine and cigarettes. R.J. Reynolds spent over $1 billion developing Eclipse and Premier. These were cigarette replacement products – heated smokeless tobacco. Users would inhale the vapors but not the smoke. Until vaping came along, these replacements were mostly rejected by the consumer.

For the record, vaping is not the same as cigarettes. It does not provide the pleasure of an actual smoke. It may be safer, but not totally safe, and is not as enjoyable.

Despite this apparent failure of finding an alternative to the cigarette, Philip Morris is conducting an international marketing campaign, "Unsmoke Your World," to get everyone to stop smoking in favor of alternatives. The website, https://www.unsmokeyourworld.com/en/, begins with the statement, "Quitting cigarettes and nicotine altogether is actually the best choice any smoker can make." Yet, the company has been heavily criticized for continuing to sell their products. That's logical, but so is Philip Morris's retort that their competitors would take over their business, sell to their customers, and then they would not have the money to develop the safer alternatives.

Now I must correct, or clarify, something I just wrote. As I mentioned previously, there is, in fact, an alternative to cigarettes, a different type of cigarette. And this story is hard to believe:

There is a new cigarette manufacturer that cannot only advertise their products in the way other tobacco companies in the United States are not permitted, but has even obtained FDA approval for their advertising campaigns and their actual product! Why? What makes this cigarette different from all other cigarettes? The manufacturer has reduced the amount of nicotine in their cigarettes, and the FDA has given them permission to state, on their packaging, that their cigarettes will help smokers stop smoking or to smoke less. In other words, the FDA has allowed the manufacturer, New Century Brands, part of 22nd Century Group, to claim in their marketing materials that their brand of cigarettes, not vapes, but a product named "VLN," and are real cigarettes, has health benefits!

According to the company's website, https://www.xxiicentury.com/tobacco-franchise/vln, VLN cigarettes have 95% less nicotine than conventional cigarettes.

Of course, this is so outrageous that there is no need for the company to pay for advertising. The press takes care of that for them for free. The April 14, 2022 headline in Crain's Chicago Business reads, "The people making these cigarettes want you to smoke less." Don't believe me? You'll find additional links under "Sources."

So not only do they get free advertising from newspapers, but they also have a one-page website, a landing page, www.tryvln.com, where you can go, set up an account, and they may very well send you samples of their products.

What is so unbelievable is that, while there may very well be 95% less nicotine in a VLN cigarette than in a regular smoke, there is still arguably the same amount of tar and other toxic ingredients. As noted, tar and carbon monoxide are what kill; nicotine only addicts. So, if a person who smokes a VLN needs the same "kick" that they get from a regular cigarette, that means they will smoke more VLN cigarettes, perhaps substantially more, to get their fix, and, at the same time, they will be ingesting substantially more tar and carbon monoxide into their bodies. So where is the health benefit? Smokers would be better off with more nicotine and less tar and carbon monoxide. To be cynical, VLN may simply be trying to get people hooked on their product and, with the low nicotine, consumers will purchase more of their cigarettes.

This is analogous to someone, use to drinking beer with a 5% alcohol content, who starts drinking beer with a 2.5% content. They will simply drink twice as much beer to get the "kick" they want. They gain nothing from drinking a can or bottle of beer with less alcohol, and lose by drinking twice as much of the rest of the contents of beer which may be bad for them in that volume.

Fourth, there are plenty of reasons why people buy a product besides the influence of advertising. Yes, tobacco is addictive because of the nicotine, but what about sugar, fat and even technology? Do we buy because we saw an advertisement or, already knowing of the existence of the products, do we buy to fill a need?

Fifth, advertising is not only about attracting new customers to a brand. It can be about trying to get customers to switch from one product to another. Take cereal, for example. No company advertises to convince people to have cereal for breakfast. That is a given. They advertise to get the consumer to buy – continue to buy or begin to buy – their cereal. And, sometimes, they compete with themselves trying to get the consumer to continue to buy from them, but just a different product.

And sixth, not being able to advertise does not translate into fewer sales. The entire history of modern Tobacco proves that. As I wrote earlier, people will buy what they want, if they need it, regardless of the obstacles.

So much for advertising. The next regulation was on the product itself.

Where? To Whom? What?

The government's decided where tobacco products could not be sold, to whom they could not be sold, and what could not be in them. At first glance, this all appears to be the very definition of an industry killer.

The government is telling everyone that they can't buy tobacco products except in acceptable locations and only if they are above a certain age. The products cannot contain menthol. The companies cannot use product descriptors. The products cannot contain certain flavors. But again, if these rules apply to everyone, it keeps the playing field level, so no one has an advantage or disadvantage.

Permit me an aside, albeit an important aside: The main ingredient of a cigarette is, of course, tobacco. What separates cigarettes is the quality of the tobacco. In the US, the Burley leaf is mostly used to create that famous "American Blend." It is heavy and harsh, but has a wonderful flavor and provides a deep and satisfying smoke. Since it is harsh, additives were added for flavoring such as orange, cinnamon, and chocolate, but not to appeal to children as was falsely claimed. Marlboro Lights, one of the most popular cigarettes with women, were cocoa flavored.

On the other hand, in Britain & Canada, they use the Virginia leaf (ironic, if you think about it!)

which is finer and smoother than the American counterpart, and doesn't require the same amount of flavoring to dampen the harshness.

In any event, all of the rules I have mentioned really do constitute regulation. So, even if there was no MSA in the United States, since the FDA regulates the industry, they are actually telling consumers that it is alright to smoke, otherwise they would ban it. Liability, therefore, attaches to the government and not the industry. Think about it: The FDA would never approve a drug that killed one in a thousand people. Yet, you can smoke.

Of course, children cannot. It's a logical restriction. And it would be foolish to oppose it. First, it looks bad, but, more importantly, opposition is not necessary. The manufacturer sells its products to retailers. The retailers sell the products to customers. And if a retailer, breaks the law and sells cigarettes to minors, it's their fault, they are to blame, not the manufacturer. So why fight it?

So, the risks to the industry, to the companies, involved with the use of their product, are spread around. Someone else now takes the blame. And that someone is the United States Government, His Majesty's Government, the Canadian Government...

Regulations are not unique. Just as the FDA is supposed to protect consumers and their health, so too, in the United States, is the Federal Trade Commission and its Bureau of Consumer Protection which "stops unfair, deceptive and fraudulent business practices." And then there is the US Consumer Product Safety Commission which regulates, among other things, the toy industry. They are the ones who keep children safe from choking hazards. In other words, for all these agencies, whether they deal with toys, lead paint, contaminated drinking water, furniture that needs to be bolted to the wall so that it won't fall on anyone, etc., public safety takes precedence over everything else. But not when it comes to tobacco. And if the regulator does not stop the dangerous activity, then the regulator must bear some of the responsibility for the consequences.

Moreover, regulators protect consumers from anti-trust type settings. They do not allow the consolidation of companies if they deem it bad for consumers. That is why T-Mobile will never be allowed to buy Verizon. The regulators do not allow the restriction of competition, price fixing, price gouging or anti-competitive behavior. However, when, as in the case of tobacco, the government takes over through regulations, and is protecting the manufacturer and not the consumer, the industry wins because, again, everyone is on an even playing field and no newcomers can play!

One last point: Unlike friends in other industries, I never suffered from a recession. Government regulations, along with the nature of the product, made Tobacco recession proof!

Self-Regulation

Big Tobacco has been successful when they sensed what was on the horizon and decided to act first, slowing government regulation. They did this, for example, by voluntarily not giving away cigarettes to high school seniors and college students, and by voluntarily not advertising in publications meant for children. In the UK, they did not place ads within 100 yards of schools, and they voluntarily ensured that there were never any sexually suggestive marketing campaigns. They thus looked good, or at least did not look bad, in the public eye.

Big tech, as previously mentioned, especially social media, are now facing similar problems. They have to deal with privacy issues and underage concerns. But they are in a Catch 22 situation. If they do not take action and create a Code of Conduct, one may be imposed upon them. If they do self-regulate, it may appear to be an admission of guilt. In the wake of the FTX debacle, what bitcoin companies will do is anyone's guess. Hopefully, they will learn the lesson from Tobacco.

Private companies have self-regulated for religious reasons. Chick-fil-A is one of the most successful fast-food chains in North America. But their restaurants are closed on Sundays. They have lost no business. In Manhattan, there is what can only be described as a camera and electronics supermarket owned by orthodox Jews. The store is closed on the Sabbath and

Jewish holidays. While people can access their website, they cannot actually place an order until the Sabbath or holiday has ended. They too have lost no business. And, in many places, there are blue laws requiring most stores to be closed on Sundays. This includes malls. They too have lost no business.

The point is, embracing regulations, and taking the lead in imposing regulations, can save businesses from a world of hurt. Not everything needs to be challenged. If you look at the big picture, it may be a lot rosier than you think. After all, if it were not for regulations and the MSA, Big Tobacco may not be in existence today. That is why I strongly believe that embracing sensible regulations is good for any industry. They will allow you to adapt, survive and thrive.

SOURCES:

VLN Cigarettes:
https://www.chicagobusiness.com/consumer-products/low-nicotine-vln-cigarettes-start-selling-chicago#:~:text=VLN%20cigarettes%20use%20a%20tobacco,help%20adult%20smokers%20smoke%20less.
https://www.globenewswire.com/en/news-release/2022/03/28/2411115/0/en/FDA-Authorized-Reduced-Nicotine-Cigarette-from-22nd-Century-Group-Nasdaq-XXII-That-Helps-You-Smoke-Less-Obtains-Illinois-Tobacco-Product-Listing.html

CHAPTER 7:
ENGAGING IN CANDID DIALOGUE

In order to adapt, survive and thrive, you have to be open and honest. You have to be candid and willing to engage in an honest dialogue with your customers, detractors and employees. That may sound simplistic, and something which should go without saying but, in reality, it is one of the most difficult things for companies to do. It is not just about listening and telling the truth, it also includes being open to other people's ideas, being willing to accept criticism and, most importantly, having this type of "candid dialogue" become part of your corporate culture.

It is totally unfair to consider the tobacco industry of the 1960s and '70s through the woke lens of 2022. For example, as we already discovered, marketing cigarettes to children had been perfectly legal because marketing to everyone had been perfectly legal. There were no age restrictions on the purchase of tobacco products. In fact, and this shocks some young people today, people smoked on planes, the subway, at movie theaters, and in libraries. When I was taking my law (bar) exams, there was even an ashtray on my desk! Smoking in public was perfectly normal. In restaurants, there were no "Smoking Sections" because smoking was everywhere. There were No-Smoking Sections where patrons who did not like the smell could sit. And remember, most egregious of all, prior to 1964, cigarettes were a prescribed and accepted medical treatment. No one knew what was going on and, once it was discovered, it still took decades for the culture to change, for a nation-wide culture to change. It is not much easier to change a corporate culture.

The importance of the Surgeon General's *Report* of 1964 was that it focused a lens on the industry. It showed how bad their products were and, more importantly, that the manufacturers knew it and withheld the information which, by the way, was based on their own research. Why did they hide the truth? They feared that they would have lost customers and their business model would have collapsed.

But because they hid the truth, they now have to live with the lore about terrible products that will kill you and, if they don't, they will harm you and, if they don't, then you are a very, very lucky person. There is the lore of the evil tobacco companies trying to figure out ways to harm the public, so they won't lose business. Proof is actually quite rare, but the lore is all powerful.

What makes overcoming their past so difficult is that the product that the tobacco companies sell is not safe. And even though they now readily admit it, it is still a very steep uphill battle to change the impression of the industry in the public eye. Even if someone goes to Philip Morris's anti-smoking website, the natural reaction will be, "There's got to be a catch!"

Things, to be honest, are not as bad as they were in the immediate aftermath of the '64 *Report*, or the Wigand revelations. Because the tobacco companies changed directions (protected by the MSA), they revolutionized the industry. And if finances are any indication, since business is better than ever, they have succeeded in gaining, to a certain extent, the public trust, something unthinkable even 30 years ago.

This all began in 1997, a year before the MSA, when Liggitt Group (formerly Liggitt-Myers, one of the smaller big tobacco companies), admitted that nicotine was addictive and voluntarily placed warnings on their cigarette packs. No doubt, their marketers told them they were crazy. Admitting that your product is addictive and kills is nuts. But what is the difference between that and Philip Morris trying to find acceptable alternatives to cigarettes for their customers?

There is none. But there is a big difference going from secrecy to candor. By changing their approach, Big Tobacco was about to stave off more regulations, keep their product legal, increase sales and see unprecedented growth. Since everyone now knows the truth about their products, they can no longer be seen as evil. Their consumers may be judged in the public mind to be stupid or foolish, but that does not necessarily reflect on the industry.

The simple truth is that being open about the dangers of their products, encouraging people not to smoke, voluntarily restricting their marketing and packaging, and trying to find alternatives, has had a positive impact. If 50 years ago I had proposed taking these steps, I would have been laughed out of the room. But that's exactly what Big Tobacco did, and by so doing, they turned negatives into positives. As the saying goes, they made lemonade out of lemons.

The lesson here is this: To take the proverbial wind out of the sails of your opponents and critics, don't sweep your problems under the carpet, don't say they are not there, don't claim liable and slander and fight them in court, don't pay legal fees to try and get your critics to shut up. Do the right thing, tackle the problem head on, and engage in open and honest dialogue. Nothing ends an argument quicker than agreeing with your opponent!

That's what Tobacco should have done in '64. They didn't. Even the MSA did not require them to do so. They finally did it on their own.

Let's consider some analogies:

Guns

Every time there is a mass shooting in the United States, politicians call for new laws and restrictions. Here is something that may surprise you: you CAN buy guns in Canada. The difference is, and many believe this is the reason why Canada doesn't have the same gun problems as its neighbor to the south, is because of its laws: To purchase a gun in Canada, you don't only need to have a background check, you also need training in the use of the weapon, you have to store it in a safe, you have to store the ammunition separately, you have to take continuing professional education classes, and you have to carry insurance. If US gun manufacturers were to adopt similar measures, they would perhaps stave off regulations, although with such a strong constitutional protection inscribed in law, the industry clearly enjoys protections Tobacco could only dream about.

Fast Food

A double cheeseburger with bacon is about 1,500 calories of figurative poison. It's bad for everyone and could actually kill some people in failing health. Everything in moderation but, if the next morning the consumer gets on the scale and sees the results of their previous day's indulgence, they may be encouraged to exercise. In any event, the fast food industry knows their products are unhealthy, so they have self-regulated by adding fruit, salads, soy, and non-fried alternatives to their menus.

Smokers know smoking is bad for them. Consumers of Big Macs know that fast food is bad for them. But they continue. Why? Because they like it.

Construction

Remember when global warming/climate change began to be a thing? At first, we were told that if we changed our light bulbs from incandescent bulbs to CFLs, it would be the equivalent of taking hundreds of thousands of cars off the roads, reducing carbon emissions and saving the planet.

The new light bulbs, I think everyone will agree, are better, but they didn't end climate change. A new culprit had to be discovered. (This, of course, is a very condensed version of the topic.) It was decided that construction, buildings, were the greatest polluters. So, what did the industry do? They did not argue, they embraced climate change to win people over. Make construction safe for the environment, and save building owners money for the upkeep of their buildings, and everyone is happy. So, the industry self-regulated, inventing what is known as LEED Certification. LEED stands for "Leadership in Energy and Environmental Design," and was instituted by the US Green Building Council. According to their website, "A LEED Building Certification awards sustainable building operations and the use of green initiatives. The main benefits buildings can experience from being LEED certified are becoming healthy, highly efficient, and cost-saving. While there are LEED certifications for new construction, renovation, and development projects, most property managers will be looking to achieve the certification for existing buildings." Depending on how efficient they are, buildings can obtain one of four LEED certifications: certified, silver, gold, or platinum. Self-regulation. Problem solved. There is still climate change, but now the attention is on someone else, which is probably what the industry wanted all along.

Bitcoin

It is far too early to know what really happened with FTX. All we know is that billions of dollars are missing, or yet to be found, and the CEO decided to move to the Bahamas and has now been returned to the States awaiting trial. Not to make light of a serious matter, as some people apparently lost their life savings, this is a problem the extent of which is unknown. Something will happen. As I mentioned, hopefully the industry will learn from Tobacco. If not, governments will have no choice but to regulate. What those regulations will be, who knows?

Fossil Fuels

Yes, they are the major culprit in climate change. But, as the United States is currently learning to their regret, you cannot simply stop using fossil fuels and switch to renewable sources of energy. There has to be a transition. Big Tobacco has tried the transition but, as we have seen, consumers do not like the alternatives. The fossil fuel industry will have to learn from the example, be candid, and grow into a provider of renewable sources of energy. It's sort of like Kodak. They refused to believe that film was on its way out and digital was on the way in. Look at what happened to them!

Being candid is not just about being honest, it is also about treating your audience with respect. You want to give them something to think about. You want to frame the discussion. You do not want your opponents to frame anything! This means flipping the debate to something more important than even health, what I touched on in the Introduction.

For example, the tobacco industry has changed the conversation. Yes, smoking could kill you. It could make you sick. Yes, smoking is dangerous. But it is also an adult choice. Do you really want the government telling you what you can't do? They make you wear seat belts whether you want to or not. Should they also tell you what you can and can't put into your body? And then what? What's next?

So now the debate isn't about the facts, they are not in dispute; the debate is about individual rights and freedoms. The consumer is being empowered with all the facts they need to make an adult decision. If you enjoy smoking, and feel it is worth the risks, that should be your choice. The consumer is in control, not the government. This approach resonates with people.

CONTENTIOUS COUNSEL

If in your industry you are facing a similar situation, you want to stir emotions, but you don't want to stir the pot, so to speak. The MSA is only for tobacco. Your industry is not similarly protected so you have to be careful. Confession may be good for the soul, but it may also land you in a court room.

It is a question of time. If you knew your product was dangerous, or what you were doing was dangerous, and you had known it for 20 years, you may need a good public relations firm and perhaps a good law firm. You are in trouble. However, if you have known about the dangers for only 20 days, you don't have anything to worry about. You will get credit for being honest and upfront and for taking the necessary steps to mitigate the problem.

That is exactly what happened in the famous Tylenol case. It was 1982. Cyanide was placed in Tylenol capsules in one Chicago store. Seven people died. The murderer demanded $1 million to stop. Johnson & Johnson, the drug's manufacturer, went public, pulled all the products from the shelves and instituted tamper proof containers and pills. In the short-term, they lost big time. In the long-term, they won big time.

Let me give you a simple example: A food manufacturer or restaurant discovers its products are contaminated with salmonella. If they immediately report it, shut down, find the source, and clean everything, they get a pat on the back and don't lose any business. If they keep it quiet, when discovered, they don't get a pat on the back but a kick a little further down and will probably have to consult with a number of lawyers including some who handle bankruptcies.

There are plenty of companies who have made the wrong decisions and, instead of being candid, chose not to communicate, to pay fines, to pay restitution, and got to engage with the government and regulators:

Verizon

During the 2018 California wildfires, despite repeated requests to cease, Verizon reduced the internet speed for the Santa Clara Fire Department. They wanted the Department to purchase a more expensive data plan. (They do this with private customers as well.) Verizon admitted they were wrong. This incident became a justification, in court, for reinstating Federal Net Neutrality on the internet.

DuPont

If you are an American, the odds are 99 out of 100 that you have Perfluro-octanoic acid (PFOA) in your blood. That chemical, created by 3M in 1957, and purchased by DuPont in 1951, is found in many products, but has also entered water supplies, including around Washington, WV. PFOA lasts forever and has caused multiple health conditions including birth defects, cancer, and ulcerative colitis. The company has paid some $671 million in personal injury claims filed by 3,550 individuals.

TurboTax

The online tax filing service actually lobbied the federal government to keep tax filing costs high, not to mention complicated. They also manipulated coding so that customers, on their web site, would not be able to find the free tax filing services to which they may have been entitled. In other words, the company tricked people into paying for what would have otherwise been free. Intuit, TurboTax's owner, denied the allegations which were filed with the Federal Trade Commission in March 2022.

Shell Oil

Shell had been drilling in Nigeria for decades, on the land of Ogoni, a people indigenous to the country. The land was polluted and, for the most part, the Ogoni protested peacefully. Shell chose to respond with violence. Thousands of Ogoni were killed, forced to leave, or worse. Shell denied responsibility for the violence but did pay restitution for some of the pollution they had caused.

Credit Bureaus

Credit reports are biased and untrustworthy evaluations of a person's credit worthiness by a third party. The major problem is that when there is a mistake in a report, it is next to impossible to correct it. In fact, of hundreds of thousands of complaints filed in 2021 against Equifax, Experian, and TransUnion, less than 2% were rectified. (No doubt due to COVID, that number was down from 25% in 2019.)

Pfizer

While we are all grateful to the pharmaceutical giant for their response to the COVID pandemic, in 2009 the company had to pay $2.3 billion in fines for illegally marketing four drugs. Basically, they had their sales reps tell doctors that they could prescribe higher doses of the medications than recommended even though they knew that could lead to dangerous side effects. The company also destroyed relevant documents. At the time, the fine was the largest in US history.

Sallie Mae/Navient

Few people know this, but the subprime loan scandal that practically crippled the US economy was not just about mortgages. Sallie Mae, which formed Navient in 2014, specialized in student loans. They have been accused of trapping students into debt, knowing full well that they would not be able to pay off their loans. The default rate was reported to be 92% and the company's collection practices were unbelievable.

Navient paid a $1.85 billion settlement. This was made up of $1.7 billion in debt cancellation and $95 million in restitution. The settlement involved some 66,000 borrowers.

Ticketmaster

There is nothing like deal making, but if your business is selling tickets, you should not partner with scalpers. That is what Ticketmaster allegedly did. They allowed scalpers, using their site, to sell as many as five million tickets. Ticketmaster got a cut. The company denies the charges and promises to take measures to stop any illegal activities.

Of course, in November 2022, this all came to a head with the debacle over the sale of tickets to Taylor Swift concerts. The site crashed almost immediately when selling began. Then, when tickets became available, they were for thousands and tens of thousands of dollars. A Congressional inquiry has been promised.

US Fruit Companies

When you are a country with only one export, you are a prime target for foreign corporate exploitation. That is the very definition of a "banana republic." Honduras in the 1910s and Guatemala in the 1950s, fit the definition. The Cuyamel Fruit Company did not like the

Honduran president, so it had him overthrown for someone more friendly towards the company's needs. As for Guatemala, United Fruit Company, which became Chiquita Brands International, lobbied the US government to overthrow the country's president. They obliged. By the way, both presidents had been duly elected...

Hugo Boss

Ever pay attention to the handsome uniforms of the Third Reich? You know, the ones worn by the SS, SA, and Hitler Youth, among others? They were made by Hugo Boss. Well, not exactly. The were made for the Nazis, by Hugo Boss' slave labor, Polish captives, and French POWs. After the War, it was determined that Boss had been a major member of the Nazi party and was stripped of some of his rights. He appealed but died before a decision could be made.

Whole Foods

It's owned by Amazon so no one will be surprised that they don't like unions. But how many people know that the company has an interactive map that they use to target stores which are likely to unionize? Using different metrics, after determining which stores are problematic, they try to mitigate the problems that could result in unionization. Whole Foods does not deny the claim and it is not a practice unique to Amazon or Whole Foods.

Chocolate Companies

Chocoholics beware! This story will leave a bad taste in your mouth. Child labor is a significant part of the production of chocolate. There are over one and a half million children in the cocoa industry in the countries which provide 60% of the beans - the Ivory Coast and Ghana. Major producers, Hershey, Mars and Nestlé, have promised to eliminate all child labor by 2025. That said, Nestlé claims that the vast majority of these children are supporting their families, working on their West African farms.

No surprise that there are bad companies. But just like people, there are also good companies that do bad things, sometimes very bad things, but still, they survive their disasters and scandals.

I want to make one final point about being candid, and now I have to clarify something I have previously said. I wrote multiple times that cigarette advertising is prohibited in most countries; that is not exactly true.

In the case of Big Tobacco, an extension of being candid is the existence of millions of No-Smoking signs around the world. They clearly tell people, "You can't smoke here, *now*!" But that also means, "You can smoke somewhere else, later." Ironically, this amounted to free advertising for Tobacco.

Who is it that does not like to be told that they can't do something? Who is it that does not like to be told that they are not able to make decisions for themselves? Youth. If you tell them they can't do something, and this is true for most adults as well, then that is exactly what they want to do. In the case of youth, since most people start to smoke before they turn 20, they'll show them, whoever "them" are, and start smoking.

This is the science behind being candid. It is simple reverse psychology. If you frame it properly, and can throw in a prohibition, you will create demand and will not be blamed because your consumer is an adult, and they made an adult decision, even if it was the wrong decision.

SOURCES:

Tylenol:
https://time.com/3423136/tylenol-deaths-1982/
https://www.pbs.org/newshour/health/tylenol-murders-1982

LEED Construction:
https://www.safetyfacilityservices.com/blog/what-are-leed-certified-buildings?gclid=Cj0KCQjwvLOTBhCJARIsACVldV2ofg1NhU39_K7nlEApJddwDjrHxu9U0GX48BQ3bK5ll41Yz8nqVoIaAonKEALw_wcB

Verizon:
https://arstechnica.com/tech-policy/2018/08/verizon-throttled-fire-departments-unlimited-data-during-calif-wildfire/

Dupont:
https://www.ncbi.nlm.nih.gov/pmc/articles/PMC2072821/https://www.ncbi.nlm.nih.gov/pmc/articles/PMC2072821/
https://www.business-humanrights.org/en/latest-news/usa-dupont-settles-3550-claims-over-illnesses-linked-to-pollution-for-671-million/
https://www.nbcnews.com/health/cancer/how-dupont-may-avoid-paying-clean-toxic-forever-chemical-n1138766
https://theconversation.com/dark-waters-what-dupont-scandal-can-teach-companies-about-doing-the-right-thing-132480

TurboTax:
https://www.propublica.org/article/inside-turbotax-20-year-fight-to-stop-americans-from-filing-their-taxes-for-free
https://www.ftc.gov/news-events/news/press-releases/2022/03/ftc-sues-intuit-its-deceptive-turbotax-free-filing-campaign
https://www.intuit.com/company/press-room/press-releases/2022/intuit-responds-to-complaint-from-u.s.-federal-trade-commission/

Shell Oil:
https://www.amnesty.org/en/latest/news/2017/11/was-shell-complicit-in-murder/
https://www.jstor.org/stable/48609133?read-now=1&refreqid=excelsior%3A10531a29c4cc07c94348b8205835a057&seq=4
https://www.theguardian.com/business/2021/aug/12/shell-to-pay-111m-over-decades-old-oil-spills-in-nigeria

Credit Bureaus:
https://www.consumerfinance.gov/data-research/research-reports/
https://www.forbes.com/advisor/credit-cards/from-inherent-racial-bias-to-incorrect-data-the-problems-with-current-credit-scoring-models/https://www.ftc.gov/enforcement/refunds/equifax-data-breach-settlement
https://www.consumerfinance.gov/about-us/newsroom/cfpb-releases-report-detailing-consumer-complaint-response-deficiencies-of-the-big-three-credit-bureaus/

Pfizer:
https://www.printfriendly.com/p/g/mqfxM9https://books.google.ca/books?id=24evDwAAQBAJ&pg=PT401&lpg=PT401&dq=pfizer+sales+manager+destroying+documents&source=bl&ots=dD6GNOrkMd&sig=ACfU3U2Uz5TPWWDJdeYqKhFLbECE53H4WA&hl=en&sa=X&ved=2ahUKEwivrfCYzYr3AhWgAZoJHao1C0cQ6AF6BAgUEAM#v=onepage&q=pfizer%20sales%20manager%20destroying%20documents&f=false

https://www.thesun.co.uk/news/15970625/who-paid-the-largest-criminal-fine-in-history/

Sallie Mae/Navient:
https://www.federalreservehistory.org/essays/subprime-mortgage-crisis
https://www.printfriendly.com/p/g/LwJbXL
https://www.nbcnews.com/news/education/navient-agrees-185b-student-loan-settlement-states-rcna12101

Ticketmaster:
https://www.cbc.ca/news/business/ticketmaster-prices-scalpers-bruno-mars-1.4826914
https://www.npr.org/2018/09/20/649666928/ticketmaster-has-its-own-secret-scalping-program-canadian-journalists-report

US Fruit Companies:
https://www.encyclopedia.com/humanities/encyclopedias-almanacs-transcripts-and-maps/davila-miguel-r-1927
https://history.wsu.edu/rci/sample-research-project/

Hugo Boss:
https://web.archive.org/web/20111108165733/http:/group.hugoboss.com/files/Study_on_the_Companys_History_Abridged_Verson_en_final.pdf
https://www.bbc.com/news/world-europe-15008682

Whole Foods:
https://www.businessinsider.com/whole-foods-tracks-unionization-risk-with-heat-map-2020-1

Chocolate Companies:
https://www.dol.gov/agencies/ilab/our-work/child-forced-labor-trafficking/child-labor-cocoa
https://www.washingtonpost.com/graphics/2019/business/hershey-nestle-mars-chocolate-child-labor-west-africa/
https://www.corporate.nestle.ca/en/ask-nestle/cocoa-sourcing/answers/stopping-child-labour#:~:text=Nestl%C3%A9%20has%20also%20helped%20young,that%20children%20do%20this%20work

CHAPTER 8:
GOVERNANCE STARTS FROM WITHIN

If you remember nothing else from this book, remember this: having an in-house attorney or counsel can be even more important than having an in-house CFO, HR director, or IT director. While an attorney is not a revenue center, they can, depending on the size of your company, save you millions of dollars and untold aggravation. As a business owner you should be spending time growing your business, not keeping it from collapsing due to silly mistakes and foolish errors, all of which could easily have been avoided had an attorney been on staff.

Having an in-house counsel is becoming increasingly popular. They usually sit on the board and serve as corporate secretary. As the eyes and ears of the company, they are actively involved in decision making, not, I hasten to emphasize, actually making decisions, rather ensuring compliance with relevant laws and regulations, not to mention contracts. The reach of the in-house counsel can extend to such things as product approvals, recipes, packaging, marketing materials, contractual negotiations and documentation between the company and its employees, the company and other companies, and the company and its customers. Primarily, the role of an in-house counsel is to actively manage risk and insurance, litigation and legal issues, regulatory matters, and investigations. Simply stated, a good in-house counsel keeps a company out of trouble. This is true for for-profits and non-profits alike.

To reiterate, the in-house counsel is not only not a decision maker, but they are also not the Sales Prevention Department always saying "No" whenever asked for approval to do something. They do not approve. They provide facts, apply relevant laws, present likely scenarios to be considered, and supply all the necessary information to make the right decision. Perhaps more importantly, they explain the consequences of making the wrong decision. For this reason, the in-house counsel cannot live in a silo, they must understand their colleagues and what they do, their colleagues must be comfortable working with them, and vice versa.

A possible example, hypothetical, this never happened, could have been if a tobacco company wanted to start selling marijuana cigarettes in states in the US where the sale of marijuana is legal. As an in-house attorney, I would have pointed out that while, for example, in Colorado it would be legal, it would still be a violation of federal law. Therefore, all deals would have to be handled in cash and the cash could not be co-mingled with other corporate funds. It would have to be deposited in banks, perhaps credit unions, which can legally accept marijuana funds. This would be an accounting nightmare and would make any profits vanish if not because of the cost, then definitely because of the aggravation, notwithstanding the public relations assault the company would have to endure.

In-house counsels can keep a company out of the poor house. Outside counsels can literally cost tens of millions of dollars, pounds, or whatever your currency happens to be. They don't simply charge by the hour; they charge in minute increments. And since they charge for literally everything – picking up a phone, entering something in the computer, opening a letter, reading an e-mail, you name it – if their hourly rate is $500 an hour, reading an e-mail could cost $50. That is why the in-house attorney must manage the outside counsels the company utilizes.

Let me give you a personal example:

When I was junior lawyer, in fact the most junior lawyer, at Gallaher, the marketing department came up with the idea of including a scratch card in each pack of cigarettes with a prize customers might win. (Think present day lottery cards.) I was not sure if it was legal, so I asked my boss. She told me that they had already received an opinion from an outside firm with which we were doing tens of millions of pounds worth of business every year. She said I should call one of the partners and ask him to resend the report. I did. Two days later the report arrived. The lawyer who sent it over had changed the date and the salutation, but it was still the same report for which we had already paid.

At the end of the month, a bill arrived for £4,500. As a junior attorney I had no authority to pay that much money, nor did I want to. I went to my boss. She told me to call the lawyer. I told the outside counsel that I did not have approval to pay the bill. He asked if we would pay half! I said we would not, and I went back to my boss. She was furious, but was also pleased. Why? Because we had now "caught them."

She suspected that this type of shenanigans had been going on for years, but she could not prove it. This £4,500 bill was the straw that broke the camel's back. Long story short, we interviewed other firms and fired the one we had been using. And this is the reason it is so important to have an inside counsel overseeing the activities, and especially the billings, of any outside attorneys.

An in-house counsel is a company employee who is salaried. They can do many of the tasks usually farmed out to outside firms. And, if they cannot because specialization is required, they most certainly can oversee and supervise the outside counsel to ensure that the company is not being overcharged and is getting what they pay for. That said, it is possible to negotiate a deal with an outside firm for a flat monthly charge or a project-based fee, even for something as relatively simple as writing a letter or a contract. Nevertheless, someone still must supervise them, and the best supervisor is someone who understands them, namely, another lawyer.

In the tobacco industry, there are armies of lawyers. That said, tobacco companies are not run by lawyers, and neither should your company. As noted, lawyers do not make decisions, they provide the decision makers with the information and tools to make correct decisions or, if not correct, at least not something that will get them into legal jeopardy. For example, they will be involved with approving or rejecting advertising campaigns. They may express their opinion that the campaign may be in poor taste and will cause public relations problems, but that's a decision for the marketing department. In that case they would be giving more of a personal than a professional opinion. However, they could very well say, and this would never happen, that an ad designed to attract 14-year-old girls to start smoking is not only in extremely poor taste (a personal opinion) but is totally, completely and utterly illegal and we will not do it (a professional opinion). Another example would be if a tobacco company wanted to start selling cigarettes in a country that did not require health warnings on packaging. Legally, it would be fine, but it would be a public relations nightmare because the company had promised to place the warnings on all its packaging. It would appear that they were going back on their word.

As the adage has it, "There are lawyers and there are lawyers." A good in-house lawyer will do all they can to manage outside attorneys, just as any other department head manages their vendors. A bad in-house lawyer will be a clearing house for farming out assignments to outside firms. In other words, they will do as little actual work as possible. The good do as much as they can and only get outside help when, as noted, specialization is required. Think of the in-house lawyer as your family doctor. They may discover, heaven forbid, that you have cancer. The minute the discovery is made they will send you to an oncologist. They will still be involved, and make certain you are receiving the best possible care, but the care will be given by the specialist.

All lawyers, be they in-house or external, are liable for their work. If they make a serious mistake, they are liable for the ramifications. Assuming there is no criminal activity involved, an in-house attorney will be fired for their egregious error. The outside attorney's personal indemnity insurance will protect them. Depending on the jurisdiction and the nature of the error, no one will be disbarred.

While outside attorneys need to be educated about what a company does, an in-house attorney must be intimately acquainted with all aspects of the business, including their products or services, so that they can advise on matters of risk analysis, compliance, insurance, and corporate affairs, and also perform corporate secretarial work.

The most important role of the in-house counsel, and if you remember nothing else from this book remember this, is to keep their company out of court. You never want to go to trial. Even if you win, you will lose. No one wins. And that is not simply because of the financial cost and the slim odds of actually seeing any rewards.

When you go to court you have to go through what is called the "discovery process." This means you must provide all relevant documents to the other side. Real courts are not like Perry Mason. There are never any surprises. All your documents must be produced. And everything you produce becomes part of the public record, including your confidential documents. Do you really want your corporate secrets in the public domain? If you did, you would not have classified them as "secret" to begin with.

There are two ways to avoid this nightmare. The first is simply to settle the claim. Everything remains confidential and the cost will be significantly less than if you lost, or even won, in court.

Second, in all your contracts include a clause that any dispute will be settled by arbitration (binding or non-binding). Again, in arbitration everything remains confidential, and you can control costs.

If yours is an international company, or if you are doing business with a foreign entity, there can be a jurisdictional issue. British companies want British law to apply, just as American companies want US law to regulate any disputes. In that case, a neutral venue is chosen, Bermuda.

Of course, the same situation would hold true within some countries. A New York company, doing business with a California company, would want New York to have jurisdiction but would settle for Delaware. An Ontario company, doing business with a company in Alberta, would want Ontario law to apply but may settle for Manitoba. Regardless, all of this would be agreed to upfront in the original contract.

In many cases, a grievance will not be a matter for the courts but for insurance. Insurance companies may be willing to pay frivolous claims because it is cheaper than going to court. But if that is the policy of the insurance company, it may be to the detriment of your company because you would then get a reputation for paying any claims. That is something no company wants. The cure is to have a "no settlement" clause in any insurance policy you take out.

Sometimes an in-house counsel is put in a very curious position. They don't want to take legal action because they don't want the activity that is violating their rights to stop, but they have to defend those rights or risk losing them. Let me give you a real example.

When I was working for the manufacturers of Benson & Hedges cigarettes it was illegal for us to advertise in many of the jurisdictions where we sold our cigarettes. On the other hand, we still had all our intellectual property including the Benson & Hedges' logo, a well-known and very long standing internationally recognized Tobacco trademark.

One day it was brought to our attention that a very famous British band had published a new album that featured the logo of one of our cigarette brands. Obviously, this was done without our permission. On the other hand, it was free advertising worth millions. Sales were going through the roof. It was great for sales, but a nightmare for the legal department. We had to protect our trademark or risk losing it. So, I had no choice but to send them a nicely worded "cease and desist" letter so that they would not issue any new albums with our logo.

An additional reason you want to avoid going to court, especially against a competitor, is that it may harm your industry. In the case of Tobacco, with all the regulations, negative public perceptions, the anti-industry bodies, media, and everything else, why add fuel to the fire? And there is another practical consideration: If you sue a competitor, that raises their status and an unknown company or brand, may become very well known, all because of a lawsuit which you initiated.

In the United States, it is legal for one company to manufacture a dispute with another company if it falls under the heading of "competitive analysis" and is not in violation of anti-trust or competition law. Think: "the Pepsi Challenge." But that is only in the US. What is legal everywhere is to manufacture an internal dispute between brands or within a brand, of the same company, and use it for advertising. The best example is Right Twix vs. Left Twix. It is silly. It is funny. It is fake. It is legal. And it is great advertising.

Question: Was New Coke an advertising con, the greatest marketing move in history, or the stupidest mistake ever made? We may never know.

From the perspective of an attorney, the only heinous crime, the only sin for which they will be automatically condemned, will probably be disbarred, and may go to jail for is, misappropriation of a client's money. If a lawyer literally steals one penny of a client's money, they are finished. Protecting a client's money is their first responsibility and that is why an in-house attorney's oversight role is so important.

But, perhaps surprisingly, their most important job is to keep a corporate calendar. Yes, they should have a dossier on all the laws and regulations pertaining to the work of the company. Yes, they should manage and maintain documents, understandable documents, outlining internal policies. But their most important job is that calendar. Deadlines cannot be missed. Period. For that reason alone, it is worth having an in-house attorney.

Contracts and agreements must be managed. That means businesses must have a system in place to effectively manage contracts signed with suppliers, customers, government, etc., taking note of termination dates, notice periods, time sensitive and time critical events which need to be managed. While it is imperative to manage and continually monitor the system, it is easier said than done.

Notices need to be sent out. It must be known in advance when executive orders or legislation are due to expire, and when intellectual property rights must be renewed. Corporate documents must be filed, along with regulatory documents. If all this is done properly, it can save the company millions. Done improperly, it can cost the company, well, the company!

Most good managers think about the obvious – employee rights, health and safety. They don't think about anti-trust and competition law. They don't think about what problems they can get into just speaking with their competitors. That is why having an attorney on-hand is crucial.

The operation of any business incurs liability and responsibility. Companies do not get into trouble when they make an honest mistake, but rather when they are not taking an active role in preemptive protective measures, by which I mean, doing what needs to be done before it needs to be done. Of course, you must know in advance what needs to be done. Telling a judge, "Sorry, I didn't know. No one told me," won't fly in court.

Let me give you a hypothetical example:

A FedEx driver on his lunch breaks hits and kills someone. FedEx will be sued because they are vicariously liable for the actions of their employees. Their position in court will be terrible if they cannot provide proof that the driver underwent proper training. If FedEx had all their policies and procedures in place, everything documented, and the driver signed off on everything so there was no doubt that he, or she, knew the rules and had had the proper training, legally, the driver "went off on a frolic on their own." While FedEx will still be liable for the accident, the damages they will have to pay will be a lot less than if they had not followed common sense practices. They will be able to prove that they were not negligent, and they will not have to pay punitive damages. As a company, you are vicariously liable for the actions of your employees while they are acting in the course of their employment. You can mitigate that liability by not being stupid. That, at the end of the day, is the job of the in-house attorney, to stop you from being stupid.

CHAPTER 9:
YOUR MOST IMPORTANT ASSET: YOUR EMPLOYEES

All things being equal, and they never are, employees will only remain with an employer if they are proud to work for them (or at least not ashamed).

It is safe to assume that no industry has had worse press than the tobacco industry. And rightly so. As I have stated, and as the industry has publicly admitted for decades, the tobacco industry sells products which are unsafe and may kill. That is not exactly a recipe for friendly conversations with neighbors, not to mention some friends and family, let alone the media.

What made matters worse was that in the 1990s, commercials were running declaring that persons who worked for tobacco were evil and wicked. Forget about the commercials, that was also what they taught my daughter in school in the 2010s!

One day, my ten-year-old came home from school rather upset. There had been a school assembly promoting an anti-smoking campaign. Such a campaign was proper, but this one went too far. The students were told that the people who worked for the tobacco industry were "evil" and "monsters" who were intentionally trying to addict children to the poison they were selling and to kill people. (This was in addition to the television ads – you can find them on YouTube – that carried the same message.) That was the message my daughter was being taught in school. Thankfully, she knew the truth. The employees of the tobacco industry were not, and are not, neither evil nor monsters. They put in an honest day's work, in an industry that is 100% legal. Yet to this day, we are vilified.

People would ask me, including family members, "How can you work for the tobacco industry?" They said I should be ashamed of myself. I responded that I was a family guy, with a wife and two children. I pay my bills; I show up for work; I pay my taxes; I am just defending my client. Many people shared the negative connotation of the industry. They were critical of my work and considered me, in some way, the devil incarnate.

On the other hand, and this was in Europe not North America, in business and social settings people were interested in the business, not critical of it, per se. In fact, there came a point where my wife forbade me from telling people, at dinner parties, that I worked for Tobacco. This was not because I would be vilified but because I would become the center of conversation. That was how great the interest in the industry was.

Some people thought I was going to lose my job because of the billions tobacco was paying out in law suits. Others were surprised that tobacco sales were still legal. And there were those who thought business was terrible. Of course, there were also those who thought we were just trying to addict children to nicotine. But the most interesting question was, "Do you agree that nicotine is addictive?" When I agreed, they said they should record me. I told them they could go ahead and record all they wanted since our corporate policy was that nicotine was addictive, smoking kills, and you shouldn't smoke. Of course, that was not the reply they expected.

I pointed out to these critics that they were basing their assumptions on what had been going on in the '70s, '80s and, to a lesser extent, the '90s. I had entered the industry at the start of the new millennium. I had never worked for a company that had secrets, that was intentionally spiking their cigarettes with nicotine, or anything similarly egregious. I never saw any skeletons in closets. There were no meetings where we discussed how to send out free cigarettes to teenage girls – as you will recall, another false rumor of the time – or how to market our products to children, or how to find an illegal channel to advertise. It may sound strange, and you may laugh when I tell you this, but tobacco companies exercise extreme corporate responsibility; they are highly regulated by government; make a lot of money for government; and are very closely monitored by government, international organizations, anti-smoking lobbies, the media, and the public, so an

Enron or WorldCom (dare I add an FTX?) could never happen in Tobacco. There is no dark side to Tobacco because, unlike other industries and corporations, there is a very bright light shining on Tobacco from ALL angles, so there is no "dark side."

The fact remains, Tobacco employees are hardworking people, who break no laws, put in an honest day's work, and then go home to their families who they are able to support and who want for nothing. But to critics, this was irrelevant. Cigarettes kill. The people who are involved with their manufacture and sales are killers. The math is simple. The truth is a little more complicated, but no one wants to hear the truth.

Needless to say, in this atmosphere, it would seem to be difficult to retain employees. But the fact of the matter is, employee retention in Tobacco is extremely high, higher than most, if not all, other industries. Why? Because Tobacco knew, and knows, that in order to keep their employees they have to treat them well. What does this mean? What can you learn from Tobacco? In a word, you have to look after your employees.

Let's begin with the major categories of employee benefits which have resulted in employee loyalty. And let me reiterate and emphasize, I have worked for British, Japanese, and American tobacco companies and have visited our competitors around the world. The following is true for all. This is not a culture unique to one company or one country. It is the culture of the entire industry.

Education/Training

First, we have education or, if you prefer, training. This does not mean professional development, which I will deal with momentarily. What I am talking about is educating employees about the products you make to ensure that they know for whom they are working, the issues which you are confronting, and how to respond so no one feels cornered when asked difficult, in my case, tobacco industry questions.

Let me give you a recent example of someone who was not properly educated:

One of the perks of my work in Tobacco was flying First or Business Class around the world. My companies probably spent something in the neighborhood of a million dollars or more on my air travel over the years. That got me British Airway's Top Tier Frequent Flyer status for life. Until the day I die, I and a guest, regardless of the tickets I purchase, will have access to upgrades, First-Class check-in, the First-Class lounge, and free checked bags.

Understand, that to fly British Airways from anywhere in the United States or Canada to anywhere in the world means having to fly through London Heathrow. Now one of the things that happens with Top Tier status, which some consider a perk, is that the Head Flight Attendant comes over to your seat, welcomes you, and asks you if you want anything. On a recent trip from Toronto to London, the flight attendant came over, welcomed me, and asked if I wanted anything. I could have gotten a glass of champagne, but all I wanted was a bottle of water, not to have dinner as I wanted to go to sleep, and to be woken up for breakfast. No problem. She brought me water and some bedding, which she helped me with once we achieved cruising altitude.

All fine and good. She was polite, kind, and courteous. But then she let it be known that she really did not understand what she was doing. Obviously, on her passenger manifest she had been instructed to greet me. She knew my status, but she did not understand it. How do I know? Because of the question she asked me: "Is this your first time traveling to London?"

The illusion was gone. The curtain had been pulled back and the wizard was clearly visible. If I may be permitted a double metaphor, the king (queen) was wearing no clothes. She did not know what she was doing. She was only going through the motions. It would have been impossible for me to have elite frequent flier status on her airline (let alone a lifetime membership) without ever having travelled to London Heathrow. She should have known that. She didn't. It was not her fault; it was the fault of whoever trained her. In the tobacco industry, this would never have happened.

I can't really blame them, but they are wrong. And if you do this at your company, you are also wrong. Most employers want new hires to hit the ground running. It costs time and money to properly train an employee so most hope that they already know what they need to know and will learn the rest with some sort of on-the-job training. The fact of the matter is, that type of thinking can cost more than taking the time to do the job right. In other words, it's cheaper to properly train someone than not.

Tobacco takes the time to properly train their employees and educate them about their products. It is truly a perk because it gives the employee the tools to fully understand the company, its products, and the issues surrounding the company/industry. This has a positive impact on employee retention. Why? Because educating employees is part of keeping them happy. This is done in two ways:

First, all employees have access to simple pamphlets that clearly explain how to respond when someone asks a question or brings up a false claim about the industry or company. Second, those that require it, receive a thick manual which has the answers to all questions ever raised about the industry. These documents include everything from the scientific basics on tobacco epidemiology to company policy on corporate issues.

For example, as I already explained, if someone asks an employee, "Do you deny that smoking kills?" the response is to say, "Of course not. We readily admit it. Look at our website.

Smoking kills. It's an adult decision. Don't do it. That's our public policy."

The goal is to stop misinformation from getting out. The means to achieve that goal is through education. But mistakes can be made. So, what happens when an employee errs?

Let's take a hypothetical case. Joe, a relatively new employee, works on the line manufacturing cigarettes. He also coaches his son's baseball team. Unbeknownst to Joe, the coach of the opposing team is a journalist. He asks Joe, "Isn't it true that you manipulate the amount of nicotine in tobacco." Joe responds, "Nicotine is a naturally occurring component of the tobacco plant. Yes, we manipulate it but it's already there. We don't add it."

The next morning the headline reads, "Tobacco employee admits to manipulation of nicotine in cigarettes."

So, what happens to Joe? Nothing. What he said was true. He simply forgot to say, or did not understand, that the amount of nicotine is manipulated downwards to make certain it complies with relevant yield regulations. HR corrects him, and perhaps Media Relations reprints some of their materials with relevant phrases or passages highlighted.

Joe made an honest mistake. End of story. It's the role of Media Relations to make certain employees know what to say. If anyone is at fault for the story, they are and they would have to contact the paper and issue a clarification.

The lesson here is twofold: First, you always must have your employees' backs. Second, if your staff are well educated and loyal, they become part of your media relations strategy.

Food

"The way to a man's heart is through his stomach." "An army runs on its stomach." Food is important. Feeding your soldier, your employee, is important. A hungry employee is an unproductive employee. Just as children can't learn in school if they are hungry, so too employees cannot work well if they are hungry. On-site food is not an expense; it is truly an investment.

People like free stuff. Think of how fewer drinks would be served in bars if the free popcorn, peanuts and other (salty) snacks were gone. The freebies cause a change in behavior. Well, on a much larger scale, the same is true at Tobacco companies. Exchange "drinks" for productivity, and "snacks" for "meals," and you will begin to understand.

In England there is a ritual called "Elevenses." At eleven o'clock, many are offered a hot cup of tea and a biscuit. It is a pleasurable interruption to a busy day. It puts a smile on employees' faces. Given the profit margins of tobacco companies, the cost is miniscule. You might even describe it as a "rounding error" in accounting terms. It is an inexpensive way to make people happy at all levels of a company.

Lunch is also pleasurable. Before I arrived, there would be sit-down meals in a dining room with white-gloved servers. Those days were a thing of the past when I started at Tobacco. We ate cafeteria style. The food was free or highly subsidized. It was good and there was plenty of it. You could eat as much as you wanted. What's more, there were also fully stocked pantries on every floor.

I had the opportunity to judge English, Japanese and American cafeterias. I have to give first place to the Japanese. The Brits (Gallaher) offered lots of food, nicely prepared, with beer and wine (if desired). The Americans (R.J. Reynolds) provided a 100-item buffet bar, junk food, and anything you could possibly want from a hot table. But the Japanese food was superior. They offered both Japanese and Western cuisines.

As I will discuss later in this chapter, one perk was no nickel and diming. This held true for food and beverages. Snacks were always free and available. The was no charge for coffee from the machines. And the coffee was the good stuff, not corporate brown water, but Coffee House-style coffee.

Happy, well-nourished, employees don't roam, they stay at their desks working. A full belly is a happy belly. And a full belly is a great employee retention tool. In fact, in industry surveys, some people listed food higher than salary for why they remain in the job.

Family

After Education/Training and Food, comes Family. Tobacco takes an interest in their employees' families. They know when the employee, their spouse and their children's birthdays are. They throw birthday and holiday parties. (At the holiday parties bonus checks are handed out along with a signed card by the company president.) Children are always invited and presents, not just on birthdays but also on holidays, are not generic. It is not a ball for the boys and a doll for the girls. They take the time to find out about the children's interests and buy them toys that they will actually appreciate.

But they do more. For example, even though I was only working for Gallaher for less than a year, my soon-to-be wife and I received a marriage "bonus," i.e., money, three weeks paid vacation to go on a honeymoon, an expensive present, and dinner at an expensive restaurant with the entire Legal Department. And this was nothing special. It was the norm.

The idea was to make employees and their families feel like they were all part of the company. The HR computer system, to which all bosses had access, included the names of employee spouses and children. This meant that whenever anyone met with a manager, the manager could ask about the spouse and children by name. Of course, it was not real. They did not know the names. And they probably forgot them a minute after the employee left their office. But it was, nevertheless, nice. It was thoughtful.

Let me give you another example of nice: One day, out of the blue, the boss told me I should take half a day off to celebrate my daughter's birthday. He also gave me a gift for her. So, what did I give them in exchange, without being asked? I made certain all my work was completed to cover the paid time off.

Think about it this way: HR, in the tobacco industry, is a managed concierge service, looking out for employees and their families. There was no work-life balance problem in Tobacco, insofar as I experienced it.

Mental and Physical Health

Today it is in vogue. In the tobacco industry, it always was.

Twenty-five years ago, before anyone else was doing it, Tobacco was concerned about the mental health of their employees. The concern was that the employees' mental state was such that they could deal with the stress of their jobs and any personal issues they might have. In HR, there were counselors to make certain employees were happy and doing well. They proactively were looking for problems. It was less corporate mindset and more sports-team mindset.

Additionally, there was on-site medical care. Even in Britain which has its National Health Service, the company had a "Health Trust." Everything was paid for by the company. There were doctors and nurses on site to provide everything from examinations if you were feeling ill to annual checkups to make sure you were healthy to injections and inoculations if you were traveling abroad. The company literally cared for its employees.

Professional Development

The final perk was allowing employees to advance and grow professionally. This included paid time off to get a degree, certification, or qualification. (I took paid time off to take the California bar.) The company was not worried that with their new skills and degrees or licenses, employees would jump ship. No. They knew they would stay and advance within the company. Why? Because of the loyalty the company had earned.

In a strange way, Tobacco has an advantage over other industries. Because they live under a microscope, with government regulators, politicians, anti-smoking lobbyists, and the media, looking for anything negative to report about the industry, they have no choice but to be certain that there is nothing negative to report. They must be totally transparent and open.

Most cigarette manufacturers do not grow tobacco leaves. Most don't own any tobacco farms, either. They purchase the leaves like the chocolate industry purchases cocoa beans. You know that great Swiss or Belgian chocolate that everyone raves about? It's not Swiss. It's not

Belgian. It is purchased in developing countries and then the Swiss and Belgian chefs work their magic. Would you buy chocolate if you knew where it came from? Maybe, but you'd think twice.

But then again, plenty of people have purchased ridiculously priced gym shoes/sneakers with, for example, the Nike brand, despite scandals about child labor. Same for other major corporations. But you have never heard or read anything about child labor involved with Tobacco. That's how you know it does not happen. If it did, it would be plastered over your morning newspaper and on your favorite news channel. Tobacco gets away with nothing, so there is nothing to get away with. Again, there could never be an Enron or WorldCom or FTX in Tobacco.

Human Resources departments at tobacco companies are run at the highest level of professionalism. They are the gold standard for their profession and their companies are the gold standard for any industry. How do I know this? Tobacco companies are union shops. The one time I participated in a union negotiation, what do you think the issues were that the union raised? Don't bother; you'll never guess it.

Because the pay and benefits were so good, and the corporate culture was so employee-friendly, the union demands were for larger portions of French fries in the cafeterias, along with better ketchup. Oh, and they also wanted more bathrooms!

CONTENTIOUS COUNSEL

So, what are the pay and benefits that keep employees happy, in addition to what I have already mentioned? In no particular order, here are the benefits offered by the tobacco companies for which I worked:

- The highest renumeration of practically any industry.
- Employees are able to buy shares in the company at reduced prices, so they feel like owners, which they are.
- Companies promote from within.
- Equal pay for women and minorities.
- Free products, meaning cigarettes. (Just as an aside, not everyone who works in Tobacco is a smoker!)
- Generous vacation leave.
- Bonuses for everyone regardless of their place on the corporate hierarchy.
- Health insurance for the employee and their family.
- Gifts to mark milestone anniversaries.
- Highest possible match permitted by law for 401(k) pension accounts.
- Tuition reimbursement.
- Maternity leave.
- On-site fitness facilities. If not available, employees receive subsidized or free gym memberships.
- Matching program (with some restrictions) for employee charitable donations. Moreover, employees are involved with corporate

charitable giving programs including paid volunteer days.
- Gifts. Most people have forgotten, or simply do not know, but sports cards were not originally sold with a stick of chewing gum; they actually were sold in cigarette packages. In fact, some of the most valuable sports cards today are those that were originally sold with cigarettes. In addition to sports cards, there were those depicting historical events, playing cards, and even calendars. Tobacco companies also included coupons with their cigarettes which could be exchanged for branded merchandise. In the case of Camel cigarettes, there was "Camel cash" which could be used to purchase items from a company catalogue. Naturally, employees have access to all these goodies.
- Managers would receive a company car, including insurance. They would also receive cell phones, and no one cared if they made personal calls! As I already mentioned, there is no nickel and diming in tobacco! That said...
- When managers and executives had to travel, we always flew First or Business Class. And we always stayed at five-star hotels. (This was true even in the late '90s and early aughts when other companies were cutting back on such executive perks.)

When our first daughter was born, she apparently had a religious or philosophical objection to sleeping. My wife and I were zombies, sleep deprived zombies. At work, I looked terrible, could not function, and was literally falling asleep at my desk.

My boss was aware of my situation and the cause. He ordered me to attend a meeting in Switzerland, and to stay there for two nights. Being a bit slow, I protested that I had nothing to contribute to the meeting and did not have to be there. (There really was a meeting!) He insisted. Then, noticing his body language I realized what he was doing. He was offering me, on the company's dime, two nights' sleep. I graciously agreed to go and explained to my wife that the boss had ordered me to Geneva and that I would miss her and the baby terribly.

Before departing, I went to Marks & Spencer and purchased a new pair of pajamas (this was how excited I was about the prospect of getting an uninterrupted night's sleep!). My goal was, after attending the meeting, to get to the hotel, take a bath, put on my new pjs, and sleep the sleep of the dead from 7:00 PM to 7:00 AM.

When the meeting concluded I told my colleagues that I was going to the hotel to check-in and do some work. They would hear nothing of it. They insisted I join them for dinner. We went to a Chinese restaurant. At the end of the meal, I stood my ground, thanked them, and went to the hotel. Instead of a bath, I took a shower, put on my new pjs, and got under the covers in my blissfully silent room. The silence did not last long.

Suffice it to say, the gods of crying children and simple Karma knocked on my door.

Suddenly, I heard rumbling in my stomach and let's just say, for the next 48 hours I was not sleeping. I had a very bad case of food poisoning. No medicine was available. The only thing room service had to offer was flat ginger ale. At that time, there was no Netflix, streaming services, or apps. The only thing I could do to take my mind off my misery was to watch CNN International (which, after a while, made food poisoning enjoyable) and watch a couple of pay per view movies, at a cost of 14 Swiss Francs each. (For the record, one movie was Spider-man. I don't remember the other one, but it was similarly family friendly.)

When I returned home, I submitted my expense account. There was never any need to abuse the account since everything was automatically approved. The only thing you could not do, if you were a smoker and ran out of cigarettes, was to purchase another company's brand and put it on your expense account. Or so I thought.

I submitted my account, as usual. My boss approved it but then came to me, apologetically, and said it was against company policy to pay for pay-per-view movies. HR was denying the charge.

I explained that under normal circumstances, I would have included hundreds of Swiss francs worth of food and drink on my account, but, since I had been sick, I bought nothing but the ginger ale. So, the 28 francs for the pay-per-view movies was a lot less than what the trip would usually have cost.

The boss agreed to my legally logical retort and returned to HR where he was told that it was against corporate policy to pay for pay-per-view movies so the board would have to decide. He responded, "I am the board. I am the company's general counsel and board secretary!" But HR insisted and he had to take the matter up with the board.

He did. Imagine this: The Board of Directors of Gallaher Group PLC, at the time, a FTSE 100 publicly traded company, spent time discussing and debating a 28 Swiss Franc charge on an expense account. It's all part of the public record. In the end, the Board CFO was adamant that I would not be reimbursed for the movies due to concerns over setting a company precedent of reimbursement for personal entertainment expenses. So, there was a little nickel and diming after all!

While these were the perks of senior management, line-workers were also treated generously. In addition to everything else I have listed, excellent salaries, food, pension, health insurance, etc., they also were a part of the corporate bonus structure. To keep it simple, every year we were entitled to a bonus. We would be paid half of the bonus, the other half going into an account for us. If we remained on the job for another year, we would receive the half for the current year and the half from the previous year.

It was a way to promote employee retention as the bonuses grew annually.

But don't think it was abused by the company to keep employees hostage, so to speak. When I quit Japan Tobacco to go to R.J. Reynolds, not only did they pay me the bonus I had accrued, which they did not have to do, but they also paid me two years' salary which, again, they did not have to do because I had resigned. All I had to do was to sign a separation agreement, which I would have done in any case.

The bottom line is, a well-paid and a well-fed employee is a happy employee. A happy employee is a loyal employee. And a loyal employee does not leave. Employees who are not happy are expensive. They leave and have to be replaced. Their replacements have to be trained. Unhappy employees leak, commit fraud, and cause scandals, all of which are very expensive. You save money when you keep your employees happy.

Thus, HR's role is simple: Keep employees happy!

Critics will ask, Where does the money for all these perks and all this generosity come from? Ironically, in part from the restrictions placed on the tobacco industry. Since they cannot advertise or market their products, some of the money that would have gone for advertising and marketing goes to employee perks or put differently, employee retention.

Pay your employees well and provide them with excellent benefits and you will have no problems with employee retention. That is, with one additional caveat: You have to treat them well.

The tobacco industry is in a curious situation. When it comes to employee relations, they strive to be the gold standard in the corporate world. They are more "woke" than the wokest of companies. It is part of their corporate culture. They fully recognize and support LGBTQ+ employees. They foster diversity in all its forms. And no doubt to make certain another Jeffrey Wigand does not appear, they have a robust whistleblower policy. If anyone, anywhere in the company, sees something they think is wrong or illegal, there is a process in place for the concern to be reported, anonymously or not, without any fear of retaliation or retribution. Nor could there be. Just think of the media frenzy that would ensue if a whistleblower was punished. It will never happen. Reporting concerns is not only permitted, but also, as a matter of policy, strongly encouraged. Dialogue with employees is taken seriously. And when employees know that they are being listened to, they are happy.

Of course, there are always sceptics. So, let me ask two questions which prove the point: First, how many tobacco employees lost their jobs during COVID? Answer: Not many. Second, how many tobacco companies took advantage of COVID-related government grants to keep employees on their payroll? Answer: None. Tobacco companies really do protect their employees. (Just to clarify, tobacco retailers did receive PPP grants, but not manufacturers. While they were eligible, none applied.)

I am certain some of you are asking, why have we not heard any of this before? It is because of regulations against advertising. If R.J. Reynolds were to publish a full-page ad in support of a minority community, never mentioning smoking or cigarettes, they may very well be hauled into court for violating the ban on cigarette advertising.

Their attorneys would point out to the judge that no regulation was violated, and all that the ad did was to support the minority group as part of the company's policy of supporting diversification. And the judge would agree.

Then the regulators would tighten the regulations due to what is called "purpose and effect" and "spirit." In other words, the "purpose and effect" of the ad, and its "spirit," were to promote a tobacco company which, *ipso facto* means promoting their products, i.e., cigarettes. Meaning it is, at the end of the day, a cigarette ad and is therefore illegal.

A company and its product(s) are only as good as their employees. The only reason a business is profitable is because of its employees. Be good to your employees and they may just be better to you.

SOURCES:

PPP Grants:
https://www.tobaccolawblog.com/2020/04/paycheck-protection-program-loans-for-tobacco-hemp-and-marijuana-businesses/
https://www.cnn.com/projects/ppp-business-loans/search?industry=453991&page=1&limit=50

CHAPTER 10:
ALWAYS MANAGE YOUR RISK. ALWAYS

The sad reality of the second decade of the 21st century is that many businesses have had to make changes to their business models in the new post-COVID world. Supply chain issues, political and social disruptions, and new environmental mandates are changing the way businesses operate and how the public views them.

The pace of change has made it imperative that companies take a close look at their risk management programs. If they don't have a program, they need one, and if they do have one, they must review and update it for the modern challenges they are and will be facing.

Risk management failures at the corporate level are often depicted as a result of an unfortunate event, reckless behavior by corporate executives, or bad judgement by boards, corporate executives or management. All that is true, but analysis shows that many risks are due to systematic problems that could have been avoided if the companies had a more robust, proactive, outward looking, and ongoing risk management program.

So, what is "risk management?" I define it as unforeseen threats that can have a catastrophic impact on a business if owners do not carefully plan and manage potential threats, whether they be financial, operational, or global health. Not all risks are created equal. Some are actually worth the reward and are essential to business growth. As they say, "No pain, no gain." For business, just substitute "risk" for "pain." Of course, only a fool doesn't stop their workout when the pain is significant. That's how bodies get hurt. By the same token, only a fool does not stop their actions if the risk becomes too significant. That's how businesses go broke.

The question we must consider is, How does a company prepare for the countless number of threats they will face, all of which have varying scope and severity? If a company follows a standardized process for assessing, managing, and monitoring risk, that can help them manage their risk.

I have three risk management techniques that I have learned for managing all potential threats. They are also valuable for creating alternative solutions where the business can reap the rewards of keeping ahead of carefully assessed risk. These techniques can make a business more resilient, stay on track, and ensure that every risk is evaluated, those which it will face in the present and those which it will confront in the future.

Management Technique 1: Knowledge

To have a successful risk environment, a business must have a thorough knowledge of all the potential hazards and threats it is facing, or it could face. It is also important to decide how much risk is acceptable, what measures the company will put in place to manage the risks, and what resources the company is willing to invest in monitoring risks. All of this needs to be written down just like any other policy.

The tobacco industry has used three steps for determining and managing risk:

The first is to assess the risk, meaning to identify and analyze the impact of future events. The assessment is further broken down into 3 subsets – identifying the threat, analyzing its impact, and determining the likelihood of its occurrence.

Identifying Threats. In risk management, the first and most crucial step is to identify the dangers to the company. Risks and their complexity are constantly changing. Accordingly, companies must always watch for emerging trends and threats that affect their sector. In the case of Tobacco, there were risks from regulation, legislation, and interest groups. One area where Tobacco failed was in identifying internal risks, employees being privy to information and revealing it as Jeffrey Wigand did in the 1990s.

There are a variety of resources available to help a company stay ahead of their competition and avoid future risks. Belonging to trade organizations, reading trade publications, participating in industry conferences and forums, especially loss prevention forums, staying ahead of threats by utilizing threat management organizations, reviewing industry specific data, staying on top of what is happening in the industry, and being aware of sales trends, can be useful in detecting risks against a business.

It is very important to categorize threats as either internal or external in order to have proper risk mitigation measures in place. It is easy to think of threats coming from outside the organization, but internal threats such as fraud and theft of data, can be devastating.

One way that businesses fail to protect themselves is by giving employees or third parties access to their customer lists that are used for e-mail marketing. By so doing, they have potentially given a competitor their entire customer list without realizing it. Many companies look at risk and think about protecting their bank account and financial information, but they don't pay attention to the other parts of the business that can really bring them down. Secret recipes or formulas, access to intellectual property, confidential documents, customer data and the like, must be properly maintained. In the wrong hands it could destroy a business.

That is why it is imperative to make certain to include threats and risks from all areas of an organization, of which there are a number:

Health and safety risks include not just slips, trips, and falls, but global pandemics. Operational risks focus on employee errors and data breaches. Financial risks can be interest rate fluctuations, the availability of credit, and market problems. Strategic risks include competitive pressures and shifts in consumer demand. Regulatory risks focus on changes in laws, the way a business sells and markets its products, and, for that matter, even if it is allowed to sell its products at all.

A relatively new risk is data privacy laws. In the past decade companies have faced huge fines for their violation. In the case of companies operating in the European Union, they must ensure that their activities are in accordance with the General Data Protection Regulation, or GDPR.

Most, or at least too many businesses, are focused on cyber threats and competition. While real, they are also external. Of course, they cannot be ignored, but I believe some businesses spend too much time on them while ignoring internal threats. For example, they don't have keyman insurance to compensate them if a "key" employee dies. And some do not take the proper measures to protect intellectual property.

In the case of the latter, this is not just a mistake made by small companies. Most people do not know this, but Marlboro is not a global trademark. Marlboro in Canada is not owned by Philip Morris, but by British American Tobacco, because Philip Morris did not properly protect its trademark. Philip Morris owns the Marlboro trademark around the globe, but not in Canada. The moral is, don't just think about external risks; internal risks can be even more devastating.

Identifying the likelihood of the occurrence of the threat. When considering the impact of any one threat, two factors must be considered: likelihood and outcome. The likelihood is how probable is it for the risk event or threat to occur. The outcome is what would be the overall ramifications to the business if the threat occurred. No matter how similar, all threats should be evaluated for their unique combination of occurrence and outcome likelihoods.

It is important to maintain a balance between the two and to consider them when weighing the likelihood of the threat happening, for example, the threat of an intellectual property registration running out. That can be a huge problem. The ramifications for the business could be catastrophic if the business is based on intellectual property. Consider what would happen if Heinz lost the trademark to its ketchup. It would be absolutely catastrophic. But the likelihood of it happening is exceedingly low because they have in place safeguards and armies of lawyers to ensure that that never happens.

Identifying impact of the threat using a heat map or threat matrix. Each threat needs to be rated on its potential likelihood and outcome severity on a scale of one to 10, with one being the lowest and 10 being the highest. Identifying the threat impact will help determine how to prioritize risk management strategies. Threats can be categorized in terms of business, technical, or high vs. low impact, whichever is more beneficial to the business. It's about looking at this on an ongoing basis and identifying the impact based upon where the threat is and where your business is at that time.

Management Technique 2: Four Management Buckets

The tobacco industry's second step for determining and managing risk is, management. When managing risk there are four buckets which need to be addressed:

The first is to recognize that some risks are not worth the risk. A business acquisition may be too risky. In that case, simply remove the threat or abandon the activity. If advertising a tobacco product is completely illegal, it is not worthwhile to find a way to legally advertise in order to gain a competitive advantage over other tobacco companies. The risk of getting caught, and the fines associated with it, are not worth it. Considering the EU's GDPR, a company may have the greatest customer data base in the world but if it is not managed according to the rules, the company will be committing illegal acts by advertising or marketing to people to whom they do not have permission to market. The fines associated with that could be devastating. In the case of the GDPR, for example, if a company uses one list with ten thousand names, it will not be fined once per list, but once per name. That is how "bankruptcy" is spelled in Brussels!

Anti-competitive behavior is probably one of the biggest areas of corporate fines in the present day. Getting involved with price fixing or bid rigging, or abusing a dominant position may not seem like the same illegal activity as spiking cigarettes with nicotine or illegal advertising, but breaches of competition law in Canada, the UK and EU, or anti-trust law in the US, can result in fines of up to debilitating percentages of global turnover. In the EU that translates to hundreds of millions of euros.

Penalties evolve. While mostly unique to the United States, punitive damages for negligence, if not illegal activities, may become a global legal phenomenon. In the US, it generally started with the Ford Pinto case. The cars had the nasty habit of exploding if involved in a side impact collision. Ford knew about the problem but figured it would cost less to pay compensation to the victims than to recall all the cars and fix them.

The court did not buy it. They ruled that punitive damages had to be imposed because the fines were not stiff enough. Ford had to hurt to learn the lesson. Thus, the general principle was established that damages need to be quantified. With punitive damages there is no uniform measurement for punishment. In other words, a company can't know what their negligence will cost them. All they know is that the end result will be severe pain in the pocketbook.

The key advantage of avoiding risk is that it eliminates the possibility of suffering losses by stopping any threat against your company altogether. But, as I already noted, no risks also mean no rewards. That is a calculation a business owner must make. Avoiding risk is a strategy of last resort after having exhausted other risk mitigation strategies and finding that the risk level is just too high to take.

The second bucket is risk acceptance. In certain circumstances, it is sometimes best to accept small threats to your business. If you do not want to mitigate them, look for simple, low cost options or simply continue with business as usual. The advantage of accepting risk is that there are no costs, and it frees up your budget for higher priorities, including dealing with more severe threats. Just be sure to continue monitoring even the smallest of risks and hazards to your business to reduce the chance of any unwanted surprises down the road.

Tobacco, for example, accepted the risk of selling an inherently dangerous product. For them, the risk was acceptable. There are always ways to interpret laws and regulations and being completely squeaky clean isn't always going to get your business ahead. There is always a level of risk. Otherwise, you probably could not sell any product or move forward with any business. If a business has anticipated or assessed that there is a risk and has decided to accept the risk, they must make sure to continue to monitor it even if it is the smallest of risks or hazards. That way if the risk changes, and especially increases, it does not become a problem.

Tobacco has done this through self-insurance. Many insurance companies do not want to insure a tobacco company. Other businesses may also be uninsurable, or the cost of insurance may be prohibitively high, because the product the company is selling is deemed too risky, even if in reality it isn't truly that risky. Self-insurance simply means putting money aside that would have been spent on insurance so the company will have that money available if a problem arises.

The third bucket is transferring risk to third parties. Buying insurance is the opposite of gambling; it's hedging your strategy by getting someone else to take on the risk and paying out if there is ever a claim against your business. You can transfer financial risks by buying futures contracts, derivates, pre-pay for goods and services or other commodities, or pool the risk with other people in the industry so everyone faces the same problem if the risk spreads. If any member of the group were to suffer a loss, everyone can contribute to the restitution. This is similar to self-insuring.

The tobacco industry has transferred risk by leaving the United States to conduct the bulk of their global business in third party countries. Philip Morris and British America Tobacco moved their corporate seats for their global businesses outside the US so that, should the worse happen, bringing down their businesses in the US, it won't bring them down in the rest of the world. Philip Morris also did what is called a "demerger," creating Philip Morris USA which is a completely different company from PMI, Philip Morris International, based in Lausanne, Switzerland.

When a company does this, as we said earlier when discussing taxes, transfer charges and capital gains taxes have to be paid, so it is expensive. But it can be worthwhile.

The fourth and final bucket is mitigating the risk. A company can decide to mitigate or reduce risk to minimize the damage in case the risk does occur. For example, they can provide incentives for clients to pay invoices in advance, by offering a 10% discount for early payment. They can also arrange short-term credit with their bank, so they won't have to worry about running out of money if payments are late.

Businesses mitigate risk so they can continue to conduct business activities that are essential to business growth while having measures in place to protect the business. Tobacco employs transfer pricing while attempting to bring different products to market to interest customers in other tobacco products if cigarettes should be made illegal.

Another example from Tobacco, which may surprise many, is due to the fact that not every country mandates health warnings on cigarette packages and advertising. Nevertheless, tobacco companies print the warnings to mitigate the risk of future lawsuits. Being open about dangers is part of risk management strategies.

Management Technique 3: Effective Systems

I now want to turn our attention back to risk management techniques. The primary technique, monitoring risk, we have already touched upon. The important thing to note is that risk management is an ongoing process. It is essential that companies maintain a risk monitoring strategy. New risks constantly emerge, existing risks may grow or change in size or scope. It is important to continue to monitor risk, reassess threats, and apply lessons learned to become more adaptable, more proactive, or more agile in response to hazards and risks facing a business.

One way to make monitoring risk easier and less of a drain on company resources is to use a risk management information system, bringing all risks together in one place, on a document, to give the owner and their management team a clear overview of the risks facing the business. The way the various risks are connected to each other, the relationship between risks, and, most importantly, the impact of these risks on a business, its product and on its ability to sell its products, require the creation of an effective system which can reduce the company's exposure and the total costs of the risks.

Every year risks are growing in complexity and increasing in number against every kind of business, with unpredictable events and stricter regulation, not to mention increased scrutiny from employees, customers, and investors. They continue to put more and more pressure on companies and their boards to stay ahead of unforeseen and adverse circumstances. Formalizing a company's defense against these risks with industry standard risk management techniques is critical to combating this type of pressure, improving a company's reputation, and increasing risk protection for the long haul.

Many companies really haven't taken risk management seriously. Two steps companies think are important but don't keep on top of are, first, they don't have an effective contract management system. As I dealt with this earlier when we discussed intellectual property, I will proceed to the second item, poor governance.

When governance and policies are not followed it is a recipe for disaster. Citibank, for example, in August 2020, mistakenly wired a loan payoff to Revlon's lenders instead of their own. When the incident was brought to trial, the judge ruled against Citibank because of its poor governance, specifically their controls for sending out large sums of money. The explanation for the error was the migration of part of their workforce to remote locations due to the pandemic. Citibank was fined $400 million by US regulators and agreed to overhaul its internal risk management and governance controls because of the error implementing its regulatory practices. Simply stated, they were fined for sending the money to the wrong account.

Common Mistakes

To conclude this chapter, let's look at ten common risk management mistakes companies make.

The first, which we have already dealt with but bears repeating, is not having a risk management system in place.

Second, is the creation of a toxic work culture. A good example is Facebook's mediocre response to the 2018 Cambridge Analytica scandal. That response significantly eroded its trustworthiness and market potential. They should have learned from Tobacco. The tobacco industry had to do a good job making sure their employees were looked after when negativity started brewing against the industry in the 1960s. They did a good job ensuring that there was not a toxic work culture, as we saw in our discussion of employee turnover.

When companies fail to mitigate risk that can alienate employees and customers, they are looking for trouble. Jeff Bezos offended his employees, suffering through the pandemic, by ignoring them and thanking customers who paid money for Amazon services which enabled him to launch himself into space. His insensitivity reflected poorly on him and Amazon. Making stupid statements and having improper responses that erode the trustworthiness of the company externally and within the company can be devastating.

Third, is an overemphasis on efficiency over resilience. The two must be balanced. Greater efficiency can lead to greater profits when things go well. For example, the auto industry realized significant savings by creating a supply chain of thousands of third-party suppliers spread across multiple tiers. But during the pandemic there were massive disruptions in the supply chain due to a lack of resiliency. Computer chip shortages resulted in the financial bottom lines of auto makers suffering when chip suppliers took advantage of the resulting higher margins in the consumer electronics industry.

Another example is the interactive fitness platform Peloton which moved its manufacturing from Asia to Ohio to meet the heightened demand for its exercise bike during the COVID-19 lockdowns. That type of resilience helped insulate the company from disruptions, bottlenecks, and trade wars.

Fourth, many companies have corporate environmental policies that deal specifically with environmental, social and governance initiatives (ESG). In the past, ESG initiatives were not tied to measurable results. The simple truth was that companies only paid lip service to the concept. That was a mistake. Exxon Mobile lost a proxy battle for a board seat because activists demanded greater ESG responsibility. Making ESG statements is one thing, but if they are toothless, they can have a negative impact on the business. If a company is going to make the statements, they must back them up. Put simply, if you are not going to walk the talk, don't talk the talk!

There are securities regulations being proposed in the US and UK to consider new ESG disclosure rules. Potentially, it could be illegal to make meaningless ESG statements. If, for example, a company is making statements about anti-slavery acts or commitments to the environment, they better be carrying them out, i.e., fulfilling their public proclamations.

Fifth, is reckless risk taking. What, or when, is a risk worth taking? The difficulty in answering the question is mostly due to a lack of risk data, process definition and governance. Previously, it was about committing crimes. Now it is about the softer areas of the business, like data protection and anti-competition. These are the areas considered reckless. Many companies are not waking up to the fact that compliance is desperately important to protect their business.

Sixth, is a lack of transparency. Not being transparent can result in untold consequences. Withholding of data, lack of data, and the siloing of data within an organization can create various transparency issues which are detrimental to business. Critical data cannot be ignored. Being open is very important. A transparent risk management approach requires a consistent company-wide strategy that includes senior management and a board that clearly defines the roles of risk management, encourages risk awareness, institutes a common risk language, and encompasses the various objectives and critical risk concerns of all departments in the company. There needs to be a centralized system of record keeping, where all the risk profiles and events should be established to collect, manage, and report on key risk data and, most importantly, once that is done, to manage it into the future. As I noted earlier, an internal whistle blowing process should be in place so employees can report problems. This increases profitability and efficiency.

Seventh, is the risk of having an immature risk management program. Many companies don't recognize that the pandemic has changed many things. Nevertheless, they have in place risk management profiles that are based on employee, customer, legal and financial risks which existed prior to the pandemic. They have not followed through and updated their risk management programs and risk assessments on how they are going to face the new world in which we are going to live. This is a huge mistake.

Eighth, is supply chain oversight. The present decade has seen a major rise in mass cybercrime incidents against modern businesses. If anything, this highlights the need to assess security risks up and down a business's entire supply chain. New contractual terms need to address cyber insurance requirements, data destruction practices, and destruction verification. Companies that don't regularly review existing agreements and consistently communicate new requirements for protecting themselves against cybercrime across their business units, can often result in devastating consequences and major problems with customers and contractors.

Ninth, is the lack of security controls. Many control systems like the Sarbanes–Oxley Act (SOX) of 2002 in the United States, and the Information Commissioner's Office (ICO) requirements in the UK, have instituted standards and regulations that have changed the ways companies impose controls and workflow processes within their companies, but the pandemic has changed all that. With many people working from home, and companies having new hybrid workforces, it is important to update security controls within businesses. That necessitates better security, availability, processing, integrity and privacy in their data, documentation, and financing which, sadly, have not kept pace in the post-pandemic world. Security controls must be pushed to the top of the agenda, to make certain that companies are not only compliant with the law, but also audits can be compiled which are based on where their employees are located, while also protecting the integrity and value of the business.

Lastly, tenth, is physical security. Perhaps saddest of all is the fact that companies must educate their employees, and have clear systems and guidance in place, to deal with active shooters and suspicious packages. Everything else I have dealt with in this chapter allows for time to react. Not physical security. If there is an active shooter or a suspicious package, all employees must know what to do instantly, almost literally without thinking. Lives depend on it.

Ironically, none of these problems, with the exception of the last, exist in Tobacco because they have been implementing proper policies and procedures for decades. This is not because they are better or smarter than everyone else, but because they have had too many third parties constantly trying to come at them to bring them down. So, Tobacco has been a leader in managing and mitigating risk because they have had to be a leader. They have been under the microscope for so long from so many different directions that, in order to remain competitive, in order to protect their assets, in order to keep their workforce from rebelling against them, and in order to avoid being shut down, they have had to have very robust and strong risk management processes in place to avoid many of the common mistakes that other businesses are making.

On top of all of this, we are now starting to see the concept of "corporate manslaughter" charges. These are charges brought against companies for criminal behavior. It has largely been the case, throughout history, that when companies do something wrong, whether intentionally or as the result of a failed risk management strategy - a data breach, illegal advertising, salmonella getting into the product, firing the wrong people, a major accident because health and safety concerns were not followed - because corporations are not individuals but corporate bodies, by and large, what you see are companies being held responsible in a civil court of law. Damages are assessed, whether punitive and/or fines, with the company having to pay out a percentage of their profits, their turnover, a set fine, damages, whatever. That is slowly starting to change, and Big Tobacco has experienced this. Now there may actually be criminal liability for illegal practices. In the UK the act of illegal tobacco advertising is no longer a civil offense but a criminal act meaning that tobacco executives will be held criminally liable. That changes things because getting a $100,000 fine for an illegal ad that will generate millions in revenue, is worth it. But it's not worth it if in addition to the fine, or instead of the fine, the person making the decision will go to jail.

Think of it this way. It will cost you $50 to park your car in a parking garage or $30 if you get a parking ticket for illegally parking on the street. The civil penalty makes parking on the street worth the risk. However, if in addition to the $30, you are also going to spend the night in jail and have a criminal record, you'll happily pay the $50.

"Corporate manslaughter," is generally defined (depending on the jurisdiction) as a crime in several jurisdictions, including England and Wales and Hong Kong. It enables a corporation to be punished and censured for culpable conduct that leads to a person's death. To say the least, it is difficult to prove. You have to prove that the board was completely negligent and allowed someone to die as a result of the use of their product. In the US, under SOX, the CEO must sign off on tax and financial records. If they are fraudulent, the CEO can be held criminally liable. This is a relatively new and fairly untested concept.

Criminalization takes risk management up to an entirely new level. This is the new frontier of risk management. Before it was about losing your business, getting fined, having disgruntled employees, losing market share. But that's all civil. When you start talking about criminal, going to jail, now you have a completely different way of looking at things and priorities or, if you will, measuring and managing risk.

CHAPTER 11: COPING WITH STRESS

Like anyone else, I can get rattled. Some things bother me. It's called being human. That said, I consider myself to be a relatively calm person, especially in business situations. This personality trait can be of tremendous value, especially in business situations, where it is imperative not to show your cards, to take time to consider your next move, in other words, not to jump to conclusions and into the deep end of the pool without knowing what you are getting yourself into, for example, an empty pool.

Despite what you might still think, even though you have read the previous chapters of this book, the tobacco industry is not run by lawyers. While it is true that they, we, are involved in all areas of the company, as stated, our job is only to give advice, not to make decisions. An in-house counsel's primary responsibility is to tell their client what the law is, apply the law to the facts, tell them if they do A this could happen, and if they do B this could happen. But the choice is theirs, they decide, not the lawyer.

Regardless of the size of your company, keeping cool, remaining calm and thriving under pressure is crucial for every successful businessperson. The question I will answer in this chapter is, What is the best way to remain calm at work or in any professional situation?

What is Stress?

While this is not meant as an academic work, I think it is important to define what I mean by "stress." Stress is whatever causes you to lose your focus, whatever causes you to be distracted from doing the work you are obligated to perform. This could be anything from something in your personal life, to a pipe bursting in the office, to a cyberattack. One person's stressful event can be someone else's foolishness. Running out of paper in the printer can make some people go "nuts." Yet, the same person will remain calm when the fire alarm goes off. You can never tell. And it does not matter. Whatever is stressful for you is the stress with which you have to deal. Just because it bothers someone else, or does not, unless you have to work with them, it is their problem, not yours.

Calendar

The first key to reducing stress is something I have already mentioned, so I include it here, despite its importance, only in passing. Keeping a corporate calendar is crucial. You can't remember everything, and you will probably forget the most important and most obvious thing, so keeping a calendar to remind you of everything from the mundane to the crucial is critical. I cannot tell you how much time is wasted playing catchup which could have been avoided had there been a calendar. Having to pay late fees, renegotiate contracts that should never have been allowed to expire, losing intellectual property rights, cost money and distract from the primary responsibility of all businesses, making money. Depending on the size of your business, not only should you have a corporate calendar, but you might want to consider hiring someone whose sole responsibility is to keep and enforce it.

Understand the Business

Calendar aside, first and foremost, you need to understand the business. Generally, if you understand your business, if you understand your work, if you know with what you are dealing, you will be a lot calmer and better at dealing with stressful situations than if you do not understand the larger picture. How many people, employees (and, for that matter some owners!), really take the time to learn about their business in a way that makes them comfortable, even though they are not running the place, and even though they are working in a silo? They still may know what their company produces, how what is made is made, but how many know what the issues around the business are, where the growth is, what business is like, what the future looks like, the HR considerations, the risk considerations, the safety considerations, and the marketing considerations? Everything may seem obvious, but I always found that because I knew the company I worked for, I felt much more comfortable operating in it. It may not eliminate stress, but it will lower your stress level when you find yourself in a stressful situation where you have to make a decision, find an answer, or complete a project. If you know your business inside and out, it will make you a lot calmer. If you know what you are dealing with it can make dealing with stress easier because you have a lot of information and potentially a lot of people with whom to speak and who can help you through difficulties.

Too often I have seen people in business who did not know what they were doing and barely knew what product their company was producing. Trying to understand the business and knowing the business should bring less stress upon you.

Keep Your Perspective

It is wrong to compare one person's misery to another. I am not doing that now. But I would hazard to guess that few people have to cope with the stress of people saying to them, almost on a daily basis, "How do you feel working for an industry that kills seven and a half million people a year?" And that is how the conversation begins! That, dear reader, is stress!

So, how can one possibly cope with that type of stress? Well, the first instance of coping with stress is to own your own stress, questioning yourself and thinking about what you are doing. The answer, for me, has always been that I am, and was, a lawyer doing his job. Now I admit, that is a bit of a cop out. It's the standard lawyer excuse which doesn't really wash. It is not the right answer. The real answer is, just because a lot of people have a negative view of an industry does not make it bad. Just because you are offended does not make you right. As I have said, Tobacco is a completely legal industry, heavily, if not over, regulated, all of whose employees do an honest day's work, pay taxes, and, in my case, I made sure that everything was legal.

Morally, a lot of businesses are deadly and most people, through their pension plans and other financial instruments, invest in Tobacco, the arms industry or equally heinous industries. Just because other people think that what you are doing, and maybe you think that what you are doing, is morally objectionable, take a moment to consider that unless what you are doing is completely illegal, you should not feel badly about it. An honest day's work is an honest day's work. Maybe it is not as rewarding as helping starving children in deprived areas, but it is still an honest day's work.

Keeping that perspective helps to deal with stress. The public at large have a nasty habit of demonizing things that don't necessarily deserve demonization because it is usually based on incomplete information. I would never say the tobacco industry does good in the world. I say smoking is bad for you, you should not smoke, the product may kill you, yet it remains an adult choice to smoke, the government has made a determination that it is safe enough for you to do so, and that the products may be sold.

Redundancies

I'll bet a million dollars that you have more than one pen, more than one piece of paper, more than one anything that you consider vital. Why? Because having a backup reduces or eliminates stress.

Why do we backup up the work that we do on a computer? Because it can be lost and if it is, so are we! It has happened to many people, maybe everyone, once. I would like to believe that it has never happened twice to a good manager or employee.

Important systems have backups. There are redundancies that most of us don't know about, or want to know about, for example, in commercial (let alone military) aircraft. There are systems in place to protect us. Two pilots, comes to mind. Having more than one engine seems to be a good idea. Not allowing the flight crew to all eat the same meal would appear to be a wise decision.

While the systems in most offices are not as complicated as those of an aircraft, having redundancies means you are not dependent on one thing. That allows you to relax when you lose the use of something. Ever break a shoelace? You probably tied the two ends together, hoped no one noticed, and the first chance you had you went out and bought two new laces. Why? Redundancy. Now, the next time you break a shoelace you may consider it an omen that you are going to have a bad day, but you won't stress about your shoe falling off!

Take Care of Yourself

It is imperative that you take care of your health, mental and physical. In the tobacco industry there are no slow days, with the possible exception of Christmas. Holidays aside, if you work in a stressful business there are always issues to confront, letters arriving, complaints to deal with. You have to be "on" all the time. In the tobacco industry, you cannot be late, hung over, or tired. You have to be at work, on time, focused, simply because you cannot make a mistake. Errors could cost billions. You always have to be at your best.

That said, as I have already noted, the industry takes care of its own and when I was suffering from sleep deprivation the boss did give me a couple of nights in Switzerland for which, you will recall, I paid dearly. I remind you of that so that you will not think that Tobacco employees are less human than anyone else. Perfection is not demanded; professionalism is.

To be professional, you have to look after yourself, eat properly, get enough sleep, not use narcotics, and not drink to excess. I cannot emphasize enough that healthy eating and exercise are such an important part of coping with stress. If you are working at a place that seems to be moving at the speed of light, with new issues happening all the time, if you have not looked after yourself, things will just go from bad to worse. You may have to look out for overindulgence, that you don't put yourself into a position where you get fat and don't exercise. There are always temptations. Maintaining health and fitness regimes really are some of the most important foundations for coping with stress.

Vacation

Go on vacation. Europeans are more advanced when it comes to vacations than North Americans. Switzerland, for example, mandates four-weeks' annual paid vacation as a minimum. When I was at R.J. Reynolds, I may have been a director and international general counsel, but I was not on the board or even the top lawyer in the company. But, because I was in Switzerland and the company president was in Winston-Salem, I got twice as much vacation as he did!

The culture in North America is not to take vacations. That is a huge mistake. If you want to give the company your best, and don't want to burn out, take vacation days.

Now some people will say that if they take their three weeks' vacation, they will come back to three weeks' work. If that is true, it is a sign that something is wrong with the company. If they can't do any of the work that you would have done had you been there, then there are HR, management or corporate issues which need to be addressed.

If you are afraid to go on vacation because you think they will discover that you are not needed or there is someone who can replace you, well, first, everyone is replaceable. That is why there is keyman insurance. If the company has not taken out a policy on you, that means they think you are replaceable. But there is a way to put your mind at ease:

Prepare vacation notes and give them to everyone. They should include information on what you are working, what needs to be done while you are away, and what you expect to happen in the near future, just in case you do not return when expected. Sharing those notes will stop someone from taking credit for your work. Moreover, if no one knows what you are doing, no one can help you so you will come back to a pile of work. You need to be open, and that openness will help to alleviate stress at work.

Dealing with Colleagues

We spend more time with colleagues than family and friends. The best hours of the day go to the employer. The worst hours are for rest, family, and friends. So, it is vitally important to get along with colleagues. Stress can be caused by disputes at work whether it be competition, sexism, bullying, any other negative behavior, or a simple misunderstanding. Therefore, you need to learn how to get along with people. Try and get to know your coworkers, not necessarily to become friends, just to get along. Knowing their names and basic information about them goes a long way toward building a positive rapport. Always remember that people like you when you remember their name and something about them. Everyone likes to talk about themselves. Being made to feel special can pay huge dividends in having a positive work environment. When you are in a stressful situation it is those people who are going to help you. Get to know the people in the mailroom and those who work in the lunchroom. Even though they neither have responsibilities similar to yours, nor earn as much as you, they work just as hard, and their job is just as important because if they did not do their job, you could not do yours. It is important to respect them and get to know them. There is no better remedy for stress than having people at work who you like and respect, who like and respect you, and with whom you get along. It creates an environment where people like being together, enjoy going to work, and have an occasional laugh. Creating a more enjoyable work environment reduces stress. When the environment is fault-finding, gossipy, and competitive, with people trying to stab each other in the back, it creates a hostile environment, that turns HR into a two-headed monster so horrific it needlessly makes your job more stressful. This is not about liking everyone; it is about treating everyone with respect.

Inter-office Relationships

If you look up "stupidity" in a business dictionary you will find "See inter-office relationships." Nothing is worse than having a romantic relationship, let alone an affair, at work. There are no winners. It may feel great at the beginning, but when things go sour, and they will, it will lead to disaster. It may seem obvious, and many companies have rules, but having an affair in the office may cost you your job and can negatively impact others, not to mention work. It is one source of stress that can easily be avoided.

Take Notes

In any given day many things happen. Two good, decent, honest people can attend the same meeting and have totally different recollections of what occurred. People hear things differently and they forget things. So, to avoid stress, write things down. Not doing so will lead to misunderstandings. It will cause stress for those involved and others – the others being people who wrote things down and remember what you were supposed to do but forgot, since you didn't take notes. It does not matter how you take them

– on paper, digitally, voice recording, in a diary – but take them. Along with notes, having, of course, a calendar, but also "To-Do" and "Work-in-Progress" lists will help you avoid trouble and stress.

Talk

While I said to write everything down, the most important thing is to talk to people. It's the best way to make your point succinctly and in the correct and applicable tone. I am not advising to hold meetings for the sake of holding meetings; they can be counterproductive. All I am advising is to pick up the phone and talk to the person with whom you need to communicate. That can alleviate a lot of stress. (And then, take notes about what was said!)

E-mail

E-mail has taken over our lives. It is an extremely poor form of communication. Punctuation does not convey tone. Instructions can be misconstrued, along with levels of frustration, performance, and importance. Most importantly, the recipient of an e-mail can totally misunderstand the intended "tone" of the sender. While intended to correct the problem, (the "smiley" face means the writer is joking), the use of emojis can cause more harm than good because they too can be misinterpreted or viewed as a sign of the sender being passive aggressive.

Then there is the not insignificant issue of how to manage e-mails. There are two schools of thought: According to the first, answer e-mails as soon as they arrive. That way you establish yourself as excellent when it comes to customer service. But that can be a very quick way to derail your work plan for the day, causing nothing but stress.

The second takes an opposite approach. Dealing with hundreds of e-mails a day, you will not get any work done if you spend your time responding to them. Accordingly, it is best to set a designated time for answering them. You can set up an "Out of Office" message thanking the person for writing and noting that you only reply to e-mails at... and list the times. That works great, unless the e-mail is from a boss or client who expect an immediate response.

Which leads to a final matter, how to respond to e-mails. The best e-mails are short and to the point. The subject line should say practically all that needs to be said. Then, when you reply, the answer can be as short as a simple "Yes" or "No." This is a judgement call and one, like everything else, you have to determine for yourself.

One thing of which I am certain is that there is no need to copy everyone on an e-mail. If a person does not really need to know about something, all you are doing is filling their Inbox with junk. In that regard, hitting "Reply to all" should be used only in extreme cases.

Lastly, organize your e-mails either by sender or project. Keeping all e-mails in your Inbox would be like keeping all files in one folder. No one would do that. Organizing your e-mails logically, not to mention emptying your Inbox at the end of the day, will help eliminate stress.

Reread

Read everything twice. Reading comprehension is crucial in the workplace. The number of people who don't read letters, who don't read instructions, and who don't really comprehend their e-mails, is staggering. How many arguments, disagreements and mistakes have been caused, not to mention stress, because someone did not read what was actually written to them?

And then there is the opposite side of the coin. How many people send off an e-mail without proofreading it? Forgetting a word, or using the wrong word can lead to a world of hurt, not to mention sending something off when one is angry. Always wait and think about what you are writing, give yourself time to change your mind and amend what you have written. That can eliminate stress for you and in the workplace. This is my rule: Don't send anything to anyone that you would not want to appear in the morning paper. If you would not be comfortable seeing your words in print, don't send it! (I call this "*The Sunday Times* Rule.")

Admit You Are Not Perfect

My personal motto, which I thoroughly believe helps to destress, is to always be open to the possibility that you might be wrong. Listen to others. You always have a way to back out of any discussion. What you do not want to do is to turn discussions into debates. By definition, someone always loses a debate, but no one need lose a discussion.

If you always have to be right, you will just look like an idiot and cause stress for everyone. When you are seen as a person whose mind can be changed, who is not stuck in their own way, who can pivot, and who can offer assistance, you not only will not be causing stress, you will become a source of its elimination.

Respect Your Elders

Respect your older colleagues. It is not simply the moral thing to do. They have a wealth of knowledge and wisdom, and a lot to offer, even if you are above them in the company hierarchy. You can actually destress by using them and taking advantage of what they have learned over the years. They bring a lot to the table. It is rare today for someone to stay decades at the company. If you are fortunate enough to have such a colleague, learn from them. They possess a lot of value and have a great deal to offer. They can improve decision making. Making better decisions reduces stress. Like the credit card commercial says, what they can do for you, and the company, is "priceless."

No Politics

Don't discuss politics at work. In the United States, if you express a political opinion a third of the people will agree with you, a third will disagree, and, if you are lucky, only a third will not understand why you are discussing politics in the first place. The same is similar in other countries as well.

Politics only causes stressful situations, polarizing the workplace. It is no one's business what your political views are. Knowing your politics, people can form incorrect opinions about you. People lose sight of the fact that we are all citizens. Discussing politics is just as dangerous as telling sex jokes or making homophobic statements. There is no place for it in the workplace.

Discussing religion is not the best thing to do, but unlike your politics, you should not hide your religion. R.J. Reynolds is located in the Bible Belt. Residents don't just go to church on Sundays, but also on Wednesday evenings. The fact that I am Jewish, did not matter to them. What was important was that I was a man of God. They were interested in hearing about my synagogue. They cared that I lived my life in accordance with certain principles. That said, in some places, religion can be a dangerous topic. You can eliminate the danger, and stress, by simply being respectful.

Evaluations

Constantly evaluate the people who work for you. People are not always straight with each other. They need to know what they are doing well and where they need to improve. If you don't tell a supervisee that they are making mistakes, they will continue to do so. It is not their fault; it is yours. Evaluating staff regularly, even informally, will cause less stress and will even save the company money.

It's Not You, It's Me

Don't take things too personally. Complaints from customers, industry bodies, and government can wear you down. There is only way to deal with it. In my early days at Gallaher, I was a junior lawyer overseeing consumer services, the department responsible for responding to complaints. One day a woman called. She had been given my name and asked the switchboard to transfer her call to me. She told me that her husband had smoked Benson & Hedges Special Filter cigarettes, a package, every day. He had died a slow and painful death, and had regretted ever smoking. His death, and the horror of it, had ruined her life and marriage. She said she wished that we would stop selling cigarettes and die. Then she hung up. That was personal.

After that call, I sat for half an hour at my desk. I was just doing my job. Her husband knew what he was doing. If I took her remarks personally, I could not do my job. And even if she had not hung up, I could not have argued with her. What good would it have done?

What I understood was that there is a reason for everything. She was angry. She was probably angry not just at me, my colleagues, and our company, but also at her husband and herself. Just as I realized that I should not be influenced by outside factors, neither should you. Take these situations seriously, not personally. Never let the personal impact your professional.

CONCLUSION:
ACCEPT WHAT'S THROWN AT YOU

I knew a man who gave up smoking, drinking, sex, and rich food. He was healthy up until the time he killed himself! – Johnny Carson

You produce a product that is totally legal. On the other hand, you are concerned that the general public will not view it favorably. You are confident that you can make millions, but you are also worried that you could lose your shirt.

We now come to the final piece of advice that I want to share with you. And it may be the hardest thing you will have to do. Here is your lesson:

The best way to take the wind out of the sails of your Opposition is to agree with them. Don't fight a battle you cannot possibly win. Agreeing is highly effective and extremely aggravating (for the Opposition). As I already told you, whenever anyone would ask me, "Is nicotine addictive? Does smoking kill?" I would always respond, "Of course." Then, when they would reply, "I want to record you," I would ask, "Why? It's our company policy. We readily admit it. It's on our website." And that would be the end of that.

I don't know what your product is. I don't know why you are concerned that it may one day be outlawed. There are industries I can think of that may face similar public (read: voter) vilification such as energy, pharma, food, alcohol, cannabis, and sugar, but not to the extent of Tobacco. (There may actually be one possibility, social media platforms, which could face the fate of Tobacco, and now, of course, bitcoin.) And, even if it does, I doubt it will kill seven and a half million people a year. (Facebook, apparently and allegedly, knew that children, using its site, became depressed and some committed suicide.) The attack you face may be similar to Tobacco but not have the same intensity.

If any other industry had had to deal with what Tobacco has dealt with, I am certain they would not have survived. What other industry could continue in business if the price of their products rose over the course of half a century from pennies to tens of dollars without any correlation to manufacturing costs? What other industry could survive the imposition of regulations on the promotion, sale, manufacture, and content of their products? What other industry could survive attacks on their trademarks including being forced to remove branding from their products? I can't think of a single example.

And the attacks are far from uniform; they are different in various countries and regions necessitating multiple policies and the hiring of a lot of lawyers. One size does not fit all. Americans are shocked to see what cigarette packages look like in Canada and the UK, with their disgusting pictures of diseased organs. Moreover, you can't see the products on the shelves at the points of sale. If that's not enough, differentiation does not exist. In Canada, every cigarette looks, and pretty much tastes, the same.

The methods of controlling Tobacco used by the Opposition have been nothing short of war. For them, winning the war would mean the outlawing of the sale of cigarettes and other tobacco products. So far, the Opposition has won some battles, but because of Tobacco's counterstrategies, they have not won the war.

What surprises me is that voters and taxpayers seem to be alright with the concept of destroying a legal industry. There is usually little to no debate about the evil effects of its products. No serious person disputes the link between smoking and cancer. Yet, year after year, voters seem to be quite comfortable with the government further restricting tobacco, even though a lot of those actions seem to be against sacred Western principles and values, such as freedom of speech and the right of adults to control their bodies. How many adults in the West would put up with the government telling them they cannot drive their cars, eat fast food, or snack on potato chips? Yet, when it comes to cigarettes...

I don't mean to sound like Abraham Lincoln who, for the record, neither drank alcohol nor used tobacco, but you are not going to satisfy all the people all the time. So don't try. Concentrate on what you are selling and make certain you are in compliance with the law. With that strategy, even though you may face objections to the sale of your product from the government and the pubic, they may even claim your product is immoral or something similar, but as long as your actions are lawful, my advice is to take what is thrown at you.

After the 1964 Report, and all the legislation and public outcry that followed, which included physicians going from prescribing tobacco to vilifying it, the anti-smoking Opposition employed a very effective strategy which almost worked. They succeeded in changing the public narrative around the use of tobacco, changed laws, and changed opinion about the sale of the product(s). Their goal was to rid the world of tobacco. In that, they have of course, failed. Why?

First, not everyone demonized Tobacco. Shareholders in the tobacco companies certainly did not. And whether they knew it, know it, or not, except those with a pension plan that invests solely in socially ethical investments, everyone invests in one or more tobacco companies. So just about everyone's retirement plan needs tobacco companies to be financially strong. It goes without saying that many are simply unaware of their connection to Tobacco, and if you check with your investment advisor you might be shocked.

What we have here is, to simplify matters, a power struggle between Tobacco and the Opposition which includes charities, health organizations, anti-tobacco organizations, other pressure groups, governments, and companies producing alternatives to tobacco products, such as nicotine gum and sedation products. All of their actions have contributed to the atmosphere of the acceptance of restricting the sale of tobacco products despite the inherent inconsistencies between that and personal rights and freedoms.

Some things are obvious. Because tobacco is so dangerous, few protest the limitations placed on the age of persons who can smoke or hiding products at the point of sale. And most people do not appreciate the precedent that is being set when it comes to limitations being placed on intellectual property rights. And, of course, there is the fact that only a minority of the population actually smokes. But always in the background is the moronic fact that in many parts of the world an 18-year-old can go to war but he, or she, cannot go into the corner store and legally purchase a pack of smokes, let alone a beer.

It is common sense to believe that power lies in the hands of those who are in control. Who can possibly argue with that logic? It is simplicity itself. Or is it? Who knows who truly is "in control?"

As I have recorded throughout this book, Tobacco has constantly had to deal with a plethora of groups, in full fighting mode, attacking them. In an effort to control the industry, opponents use what I call "The Three 'A's Strategy," namely Affordability, Acceptability, and Availability. What this really means, what control is really about, is lowering smoking initiation, increased cessation, and reduced consumption. Tobacco as we have seen, has been able to counter each. What's more, as you will remember, Tobacco has had to go it alone. As I told you previously, when I reached out to colleagues in the alcohol industry to get them to join us in our fight against government regulations, they wanted nothing to do with us. Today, some may regret that decision.

Now, to conclude our trip through the world of Tobacco, let's concentrate on those Three "A"s I just mentioned.

Affordability

The simplest way to destroy an industry is to price its products to such an extent that no one can afford to purchase them. Most people have limited income and limited disposable income. When a pack of cigarettes cost a quarter, fifty cents, or a dollar, it was not a major financial decision to buy a pack or even a carton. The dried leaves and paper, which only cost pennies to manufacture, cost an insignificant amount of income, disposable or otherwise, to buy. So, the Opposition's first victory was raising the price, due to various taxes, to as much as $20 a pack, a price which, again, bears no relation to the actual cost to manufacture the product, and is due to, in some cases, as I have emphasized more than once, as much as 80% taxation.

That said, the Opposition was not totally successful. First, as we have already learned, when due to taxation of one form or another, the price of cigarettes increased, tobacco manufacturers simply added a few cents to the cost of each pack, the government getting the blame and the manufacturers pocketing the profits. Today, as we have already learned, Tobacco makes more per pack than they ever had in the past. That is why, even if there are fewer smokers, there are increased profits.

Second, the high taxation hooked the government on the necessity of people buying cigarettes. The government needs the tax revenue. Of course, not mentioned in polite society, but stated earlier, is the fact that if seven and a half million people die every year from smoking, that's seven and a half million fewer people utilizing the governmental social safety net, saving the government money.

Third, if the tobacco manufacturers can collect the tax revenue, and hold on to it for several days or months, that's the same as a free loan from the government which they can use to invest in their businesses.

Fourth, Tobacco was able to join forces with retailers. By raising the price of cigarettes astronomically, that made cigarettes a valuable commodity. Thieves like to steal valuable things. So, as we will see when we discuss the third "A," the fact that cigarettes are now hidden has helped, not hurt, Tobacco.

While the strategy worked in significantly lowering the prevalence of smoking, most significantly by dropping the number of adult smokers in countries where the controls are in place, Tobacco profits have never been as high as they are today. So, the so-called control did not put Tobacco out of business, but made it stronger. In fact, the controls resulted in Tobacco securing for itself a patron who protects it because of the revenue it produces for them, namely, the government.

Acceptability

The Opposition began its Acceptability campaign moderately. It was simple: Smoking is bad for you, so don't smoke. Sweet. Simple. Uncomplicated. Why argue?

Then they became a little more aggressive. They sought to ban smoking in certain places so that smokers became pariahs. Concerns over second-hand smoke were added to the mix. To a large degree this part of the Opposition's campaign was highly successful.

People have been conditioned that the control of tobacco is just part of everyday life. Facts have been forgotten. It is fascinating that people truly believe that there were once "Smoking Sections" in restaurants and on airplanes. I repeat, the fact of the matter is, that until near the end of the past century, on airplanes, in restaurants, public buildings, even hospitals, everywhere was a Smoking Section. You were permitted to smoke wherever you wanted, except in the limited "No-Smoking Sections." The proof of the change in Acceptability is the reversal from being able to smoke anywhere, to being able to smoke almost nowhere except, perhaps, on the sidewalk. (In fact, it was Tobacco that suggested building smoking shelters outside of buildings.)

The bans on advertising cigarettes; the passage of smoke-free laws; the outlawing of smoking in clubs, restaurants, bars, and workplaces; replacing attractive packaging with plain packaging featuring health warnings and/or disgusting photos; and public service announcements, warning that smoking can harm an unborn baby, may have contributed to smoking no longer being an acceptable social norm but, as we have seen, it also provided cigarette manufacturers with free advertising.

The Opposition also had another success: In movies in the US, smoking is treated like nudity, which means if someone is seen smoking, the movie is automatically rated R. On the other hand, smoking is permitted on Netflix and HBO because the minimum age of viewers is presumably guaranteed. Just as an aside, in some countries you cannot show people drinking alcohol in commercials (this is an example of industry self-regulation), although you can see them on shows and in movies.

Tobacco has no problem with any of this because they do not want to sell their products to children. Since December 2019, the legal smoking age in the United States is 21. In Mexico, and most of Canada, it is 18. Manufacturers want to get adults to switch to their brands, they don't want underage smoking which is why they have assisted retailers with age verification programs. The ironic thing about government restrictions is that some smokers even claim to support them. They profess that they want to stop, and restrictions will help them. Their sincerity may be questioned.

Availability

Finally, the Opposition also failed when it came to the third "A," Availability. In some countries and states governments poured money into their respective treasuries through licensing fees paid by retailers wanting to sell tobacco products. Age checks and limits on the sale of cigarettes, along with the elimination of vending machines, freed manufacturers from charges that they sold their products to minors. The government may have made it a bit difficult to find cigarettes, but they guaranteed that they would be there.

As I just mentioned, Tobacco and retail sellers joined forces. Now that cigarettes are an ultra-premium product item, they are worth stealing. Steal a hundred cartons of cigarettes and, if you are a good thief, by the end of the day you will have thousands of dollars in your pockets.

So, what did Tobacco do? They helped retailers build secure gantries. Today, in cities across the United States, the evening news shows thieves stealing arms full of merchandise with impunity. Things got so bad in Manhattan that pharmacies had to lock up toothpaste. But what don't the thieves steal? Cigarettes. Why? Because they can't get to them. They are locked up out of reach.

The retailers, especially the small convenience stores, gain something else. Because the price of a pack of cigarettes is so high, smokers can no longer afford to buy a carton, so they buy a pack every day or so. Which means foot traffic in the stores has increased. And if you are going to buy your smokes, you probably are also going to buy a drink, chewing gum or breath mints, a bag of chips, a newspaper, maybe a magazine. So, retailers are selling more high-margin products because of the sale of low-margin cigarettes.

These lessons, for the record, go against everything that is taught in business schools!

Most importantly, the Opposition forgot that when people are addicted to a substance, they will find a way to get it. True, there are no longer aisles in grocery stores devoted to tobacco products, and packs are no longer sold at check-out aisles alongside candy bars, gum and breath mints, but they are still available.

The government measures the number of smokers, based on the sale of duty paid product at legal establishments and then dividing that number by the adult population. Of course, this totally ignores the black market. In any event, while the volume of sales may have decreased, that does not mean that the number of smokers has decreased. So, Tobacco has not lost smokers only sales.

Availability was the cornerstone of the Opposition campaign. Even if you are willing to be a pariah in the eyes of society, and even if you are willing to spend your children's college fund to pay for your smokes, if there are no cigarettes available, you can't smoke. So, the fact that cigarettes are easily had, means the Opposition lost and Tobacco won.

Of course, they have had to adapt. Like any other manufacturer selling a retail product in stores, Tobacco wants as many "facings" as possible. If Philip Morris could only sell one brand of cigarette, while R.J. Reynolds could sell ten, that would be unfair. But, as we have seen, in countries like Canada and the UK, there is a level playing field for all tobacco manufacturers. None of their products have "facings" because no one can see them. The Opposition got rid of vending machines which made it easy for the underaged to buy the product. The machines were removed from sports arenas, billiard halls, restaurant restrooms, etc. That was a true success for the Opposition.

Another success, at least in the US, was the decision of the pharmacy chain CVS to stop selling cigarettes. In the short-term that cost the company, according to *Forbes Magazine*, $2 billion. They are expected to recoup those loses, and then some, because of the wisdom of the decision and the good-will it has garnered with customers. In Canada, all pharmacies are forbidden to sell tobacco products.

Sadly, the Opposition's Availability campaign backfired in one important way. By hiding cigarettes, they made them very attractive to young people, especially boys. Just as they want to see what is behind the brown paper wrapper of the pornographic magazines, they want to learn for themselves what all the fuss is about with regards to smoking. As noted earlier, tell a young person what they cannot do, and that is precisely what they will want to do. And, again, you cannot blame the tobacco manufacturer for this. They do not sell cigarettes, retailers do, not to mention black marketers and foolish adults who agree to buy cigarettes, and, for that matter, alcohol, for youth.

So, in conclusion, when faced with a powerful Opposition, learn from Tobacco. Don't panic, adapt. Accept what you cannot control. There is never any point in fighting a losing battle. The only thing you can do is slow the Opposition so that you have time to adapt.

In my day, I witnessed the partial destruction of Tobacco. People, friends, lost their jobs. I was concerned about my job. From a business perspective, this was actually quite frightening.

I'll say it again, the way to control the Opposition to the greatest extent possible, the way to control the destruction of your industry to the greatest extent possible, and the way to control fear, is to adapt.

Think of it as the Opposition looking for a revolution while you want an evolution. Darwin didn't actually consider evolution to be the survival of the fittest, but rather of the fitter. So be fit, and don't smoke.

SOURCES:

Drinking on commercials:
https://learningtohomebrew.com/why-cant-beer-commercials-show-drinking/

CVS:
https://www.forbes.com/sites/robertglazer/2020/04/21/cvs-lost-2-billion-with-1-decision-heres-why-they-were-right/?sh=1f8a9ea0689c

Darwin:
https://www.britannica.com/science/survival-of-the-fittest

ABOUT THE AUTHOR

Max Krangle is internationally recognized as an expert in business growth and development in highly regulated industries. A graduate of the University of Law in London, and the holder of a Bachelor of Science degree from the University of Bristol, Max is a Solicitor of the Supreme Court of England and Wales and a Commissioner for Oaths.

Additionally, he is the Managing Director of the Toronto, Ontario-based international legal and business consulting firm Counsel Strategy, where he helps businesses grow and remain competitive in increasingly regulated domestic and international environments by providing compliance services and legal expertise from a business perspective, and to implement business strategies.

Max began his legal career as a London, UK-based lawyer in the entertainment industry. He entered the world of Big Tobacco, where he remained for many years, advancing quickly in the legal ranks. He served as Legal Counsel (UK & Ireland), Senior Counsel (Europe), and Assistant Counsel and Director at Japan Tobacco International SA (Geneva, Switzerland) which purchased his former employer, the Gallaher Group PLC (London, UK). He then advanced to become the General Counsel and Senior Director of R.J. Reynolds Global Products, Inc. in Zurich, Switzerland and Winston-Salem, North Carolina.

For practically his entire adult life, Max had been fascinated with cigarettes. From a very young age, he was a fan of *The Tonight Show Starring Johnny Carson*. The idea of Johnny Carson smoking his Pall Mall cigarettes on set, looked to him like the ultimate in "cool."

His professional dream had nothing to do with Tobacco. After he realized that Jay Leno would be replacing Johnny Carson on *The Tonight Show*, he switched his attention to replacing Tom Brokaw as anchor of *The NBC Nightly News*, which of course was a pie-in-the-sky idea that was nothing short of unrealistic. But all kidding aside, for five years, he worked as an intern and junior researcher for NBC News Worldwide in London, during university and law school, respectively. He was at NBC for some fairly big stories including the war in Bosnia, and the death and funeral of Princess Diana. On the radio side of the business, he covered major events including Wimbledon and music concerts. During this time, he also had a stint at the BBC World Service news department.

CONTENTIOUS COUNSEL

Max joined the media and entertainment firm Fenton Hills Solicitors in London in 1998, working mostly in Intellectual Property. He worked for the restaurant chain Pret a Manger, doing their international brand protection work as the company grew from a single sandwich shop in London to an international presence.

After three years he was headhunted to work for the old English Bond Street tobacco company, Gallaher Group Plc, in a junior management position at their worldwide headquarters based in the United Kingdom. The company manufactured Benson & Hedges cigarettes, along with Silk Cut, Mayfair, Hamlet Cigars, Amber Leaf Rolling Tobacco, and multiple pipe tobaccos. This was a year after the MSA had been signed in the United States and the Tobacco environment that had been, was no more.

Going into the tobacco industry totally changed his life. He continued to do Intellectual Property law and brand protection. He got heavily involved with sponsorship work, particularly Formula One Motor Racing. For him, it was a fascinating industry. On the other hand, ironically, he considered legal work, especially Intellectual Property, relatively boring and mundane. But he was interested in business and was fascinated by the fact that he was in an industry that killed millions of people a year but remained completely legal. He never saw himself as someone who should be ashamed that he was working for a tobacco company because, as a lawyer he had been taught, and all lawyers believe this (or at least they should), that everyone is entitled to the best possible legal counsel they can obtain. His client was not doing anything illegal, and, as far as he was concerned, he was standing up for their rights like any other attorney stands up for their clients.

When he began in Tobacco, he was not immune to the existing preconceptions. He too thought things would be clandestine. But what he found was an industry that was very cautious, and policy and compliance oriented. Everything was run through the legal department. Compliance was everywhere. As a result, he was very involved in a business which he found fascinating. There were no clandestine measures – such as spiking cigarettes with nicotine, denying that nicotine is addictive, or that smoking kills. That may have been true once, but not in the last 30 years, and certainly not during his tenure.

At Gallaher, he was their UK counsel working primarily on their business in the UK and Ireland, and various western European files (Iberia, France, Benelux, Italy, and others.) In 2005, he was sent to Lausanne in Switzerland.

It was a great growth industry not just because they valued professionalism, but also because, given the climate, good employees were hard to come by. He fit the bill and advanced very quickly. He was Counsel, then Senior Counsel, Assistant General Counsel and, finally, General Counsel.

In 2008, Gallaher was acquired by Japan Tobacco (JTI), the third largest tobacco company in the world. Internationally, they own all the historical Reynolds' brands, including Camel and Natural American Spirit.

At the time, JTI was half owned by the Japanese Ministry of Finance. So, for a period of time, technically, he was a Japanese civil servant. (Their offices were located in Geneva, so he commuted there every day from Lausanne.)

He was high enough up in the organization at the time of the takeover to be of interest to the JTI management takeover team, but not so high that, unlike his boss and her boss, he wasn't immediately let go. That made him the senior most ranking lawyer to stay with the company.

At JTI he had been given a portfolio that he had never done before. He went from being Senior Counsel for Europe to being the lawyer for Business Development. Even though he had the title of Assistant General Counsel, his job for the year and a half that he was there was to sell off the parts of Gallaher that they did not want to keep. So, in truth, it was not "Business Development" but rather "Business *Un*development."

Based on his performance, he was promoted well above where he should have been for someone his age. He was sitting on boards of directors in his 30s, with men and women 20-25 years older than he was, in different stages of their careers, laughing at him because he would arrive with dark bags under his eyes from not getting any sleep because he had two screaming babies at home. As some of them were pleased to point out, their kids had graduated from college around the time his were born!

Eventually, he decided to leave R.J. Reynolds, partially because of the need to move and partially because of a Christmas card.

He was a Canadian ex-pat. Ex-pats are paid a lot of money. They get their salary. Their taxes are equalized to make sure they are not losing out on what they would have paid if they had been working from "home." They are paid for their housing, their children's school fees, nannies, cars, everything. The object of any ex-pat is to find locals to take over and then move on to the next project. In a nutshell, that's what happened to him.

Reynolds wanted to localize the position. He was offered the opportunity to move to Winston-Salem for a permanent position. He decided not to. It's a lovely city, far less expensive than either Toronto or London, but, and this is not a reflection on the city and certainly not the people, he and his wife preferred Toronto.

(For context, his wife was born and grew up in Hong Kong. She went to high school in Rome, and attended university in Paris. They met and lived in London and moved to Lausanne. They were simply used to large cities, not small-town America.)

Usually, when International General Counsels retire from corporate life, they retire to the golf course. Max was in his late 30s. He had many years before retiring to a country club.

Due to an excellent severance package, he was able to do what he wanted, namely, to start a consulting business and, more personally, to be near his aging parents. Reynolds paid for the move to Canada, and he started his own business.

Money aside, the most valuable thing he received from his years in Tobacco was the legal experience which very few lawyers have. He has therefore become a source that can provide business owners with knowledge that is unique: He has worked in Fast Moving Consumer Goods (FMCG), marketing, law, insurance, risk management and business, and all in an international context. He was not a third-party attorney working for a company, but an employee of the company in operational and managerial capacities.

Max has a lot to bring to other industries that are heading to the highly regulated and monitored environment of Tobacco such as: online gambling, sports betting, a client who was trying to acquire the entire Playboy catalogue, cannabis, and the psilocybin and magic mushroom industry. He has also had skincare and pharmaceuticals clients. His clients' thinking is, if he could protect Tobacco, keep them not only on the straight and narrow, but also keep them profitable, he was the one they wanted on their teams.

In a nutshell, what this all comes down to is the fact that for most, if not all of his professional life, he has worked in a highly regulated, highly monitored and highly restricted industry. That is a situation which many businesses are now facing, or anticipating that they will be facing. It is important to understand that within contentious industries problems are potentially going to happen on a grander scale than normal.

The subject of the critically acclaimed book, *Firebrand: A Tobacco Lawyer's Journey*, by Joshua Knelman, Max and his wife, Melany, still reside in Toronto, with their two daughters.

LEGAL NOTICE

While all attempts have been made to verify and source third party information provided in this publication, the Author and Publisher assume no responsibility for errors, omissions, or contrary interpretation of the subject matter herein. Any perceived slight of specific persons, peoples, or organizations is unintentional.

In practical advice books, like anything else in life, there are no guarantees of business success. Readers are cautioned to rely on their own judgment about their individual circumstances and to act accordingly.

This book is not intended for use as a source of actual legal advice. All readers are advised to seek the services of registered legal professionals in their legal jurisdiction of business operations.

Manufactured by Amazon.ca
Bolton, ON

38440082R00141